Soundings

5-00

8

Issue 9

The
European
Left

EDITORS
Stuart Hall
Doreen Massey
Michael Rustin

GUEST EDITOR
Martin Peterson

POETRY EDITOR
Carole Satyamurti

REVIEWS EDITORS
Becky Hall and
Susanna Rustin

ART EDITOR
Tim Davison

EDITORIAL OFFICE
Lawrence & Wishart
99a Wallis Road
London E9 5LN

MARKETING CONSULTANT
Mark Perryman

ADVERTISEMENTS
Write for information to Soundings,
c/o Lawrence & Wishart

SUBSCRIPTIONS
1998/9 subscription rates are (for three issues):
UK: Institutions £70, Individuals £35
Rest of the world: Institutions £80, Individuals £45

ISSN 1362 6620
ISBN 085315 878 9

Text setting Art Services, Norwich
Cover photograph: © Sarah Williams

Printed in Great Britain by
Cambridge University Press, Cambridge

Soundings is published three
times a year, in autumn,
spring and summer by:
Soundings Ltd
c/o Lawrence & Wishart
99a Wallis Road
London E9 5LN

CONTENTS

——————— **Part 2 - New beginnings for a European left** ———————

————————————— *Continued on next page* —————————

Continued from previous page

NOTES ON CONTRIBUTORS

Alexandra Ålund is Professor of Sociology at the University of Umeå, Sweden. With a background in the former Yugoslavia she is recognised as a leading expert in Sweden and internationally on immigrant and multi cultures.

Philip Arestis is Professor of Economics at the University of East London.

Harriet Atkinson is a freelance writer.

Alain Caillé is a French journalist and co-author of *Le tournement de décembre*.

John Crowley is Research Fellow at Centre d'Etudes et de Recherches Internationales, Paris; secretary general of EAS and a prolific writer on contemporary social theory.

Leonidas Donskis is Head of the Centre for Studies on Culture and Civilization, University of Klaipeda, Lithuania.

Judy Gahagan has published two pamphlets of poetry and a book of short stories. She lives in London and Italy.

Becky Hall and **Susanna Rustin** are joint editors of *Soundings* reviews section.

Catherine Hall is Professor of Modern British Social and Cultural History at University College, London. Her new book, *Civilizing Subjects*, is published by Polity Press next year.

Chantal Mouffe is a Research Fellow at the Centre for the Study of Democracy at the University of Westminster in London. She is the author of several books, including *Hegemony and Socialist Strategy; Towards a Radical Democratic Politics* (with Ernesto Young, Verso, 1985) and *The Return of the Political* (Verso, 1993).

Branka Likic-Brboric is a Research fellow at the University of Uppsala, Sweden and, until 1993, Lecturer in Economics at the University of Sarajevo, Bosnia.

Angela McRobbie is Professor of Communications at Goldsmiths College, London.

Okello Oculi was born in Uganda and currently lives in Nigeria. He has published three volumes of poetry and a novel.

Martin Peterson is the head of a faculty programme on Europe, University of Gothenburg, Sweden; member of the Swedish Council for the Planning and Documentation of Research; member of the Board of the ICCR, Vienna.

Mario Petrucci, born of Italian parents, has worked as a university lecturer, farm-hand and engineer. His collection *Shrapnel and Sheets* (1996) was a Poetry Book Society Recommendation.

Carole Satyamurti's Selected Poems will be published by OUP in September.

Malcolm Sawyer is Professor of Economics at the University of Leeds.

Ove Sernhede is a Research Fellow and Head of the Forum for Studies on Contemporary Cultures at the University of Gothenburg, Sweden.

Máté Szabó is a Research Fellow at the influential research institute TARKI in Budapest, Hungary.

Catherine Smith teaches creative writing part-time at the University of Sussex.

Peter Weinreich is Professor of Psychology at the University of Ulster and creator of *Identity Strategy Analysis*.

Frances Wilson teaches, writes and paints. Her collection of poetry, *Close to Home*, is published by Rockingham Press.

Avoiding disenchantment

New Labour has found its own way of sparing those of a leftward inclination from the painful experience of disillusion. This was to devise a programme that was so minimal that it discouraged its supporters from having extravagant hopes in the first place. But our determination not to become locked in a cycle of disappointment reminiscent of the 1960s and 1970s has a much deeper root than this. We believe that the political development that we have all been engaged in, since the election victory of a May 1998, is not predetermined in its outcomes. It has been the commitment of *Soundings* since its inception to explore the spaces surrounding the formal political process, and to try to identify growing points which might shape an emergent agenda in the medium term. We remain hopeful that such growing points will in due time emerge.

We also recognise with satisfaction the many aspects of energy and competence shown by the Blair government, of which the continuing Northern Ireland peace process has been so far the most important single outcome. The implementation of devolution is another such step. It is not a negligible thing for a Labour government to have retained its full popularity, and a clear grasp of its own sense of political purpose, after more than a year in office, even though some of us would have preferred a policy script that was different in significant ways, and even though the Government's overriding purpose seems to be to ensure its retention of office for a considerable term.

In our current issue, some contributors take critical issue with the New Labour government, nonetheless. Chantal Mouffe's article, 'The Radical Centre; Politics without Adversaries', identifies the problems of a politics that seeks to avoid conflict at almost any price. The effect of such an all-inclusive idea of consensus, far from drawing the whole population into a process of democratic reforms, is, implicitly, to grant a political veto to almost any interest that can threaten the loss of some fraction of support. Unfortunately, in this calculus, those interests which speak for the power of business have weighed more heavily than those identified with Labour. We have seen a number of examples of withdrawals under hostile fire since the general election. Philip Arestis and Malcolm Sawyer's 'New Labour - New Monetarism' points out the continuities between the economic assumptions underlying Thatcherite and New Labour economic programmes. The government thus accepts its subordination to a global market whose compelling signals are rates of interest and capital flows. These are political and economic constraints which the government has imposed on itself.

These two articles reflect our continuing commitment to create a robust debate around several of the key fault-lines in the New Labour project, even though we acknowledge the possibilities that its political success makes possible. We have already published a sequence of articles on globalisation.[1] This is one key concept on which we wish to transform debate, to call into question the status of globalisation as an unchallengable 'reality' to which governments and peoples must merely adapt themselves; instead we argue that it should be recognised as an ideological construction, and as the effect of specific social and economic forces. In the same way, whilst recognising the inevitable and (sometimes) productive effects of markets as modes of organisation, we will continue to insist in *Soundings* on the recognition of their costs, and on the need for markets to be bounded, regulated, and sometimes replaced, by more social and democratic practices. We have explored alternatives to such markets in our issue on *The Public Good*. In summary, we see the role of a magazine of the left at this point as being to put in question the currently prevailing ideas of consensus, of markets, of globalisation, of inequality,[2] and of undivided national and ethnic identities. We shall press New Labour to identify itself as being -

---

1. By Paul Hirst and Grahame Thompson in *Soundings* 4, by David Goldblatt, David Held, Anthony McGrew, and Jonathan Perraton, and in an Editorial by Doreen Massey, both in *Soundings* 7.
2. For example in Richard Wilkinson's article in our special *Next Ten Years* issue of last year.

unavoidably - on one side of the political conflicts which inevitably form around these central lines of division between left and right.

Two articles in this issue explore areas which fall outside the usual agendas of political parties. Mario Petrucci examines the claims of future generations, raising rarely-acknowledged issues of values and priorities. This article contrasts, in a principled way, with the short-termism of most political decision-making. Angela McRobbie writes about the role of popular music as a key form of expression for young people, viewing music as a self-created language through which multi-ethnic identities are created and lived. This kind of engagement with generational difference is very different from the often superficial attempts at cooption we see from politicians. McRobbie's article develops themes which we earlier explored in our (ironically titled) *Young Britain* issue.

The European Left

The theme for the second half of this issue is the European Left. This reflects our commitment to Europe as a potential container for a more democratic and socially responsible form of capitalism than can now be sustained within a single nation state - still less nation states under the hegemony of the United States. The crisis of the most social-democratic of nation states provides one of the main points of departure for the themed section, which was edited in Sweden by Martin Peterson. The vision of a new European left which shapes this issue has three key dimensions. First, that it must include both western, and eastern and central Europe. Articles on Lithuania, Slovenia, and Hungary identify positive points of departure, as well as risks, from these three national perspectives. Secondly there is the argument that the growth of an autonomous civil society, rooted in social movements as much as in the institutions of class solidarity, has become the key to a progressive politics. The third and most important dimension is the need to recognise and respect the multi-ethnic and multi-cultural character of European society, if its democratic basis is to be secured, let alone advanced. In this European Left issue, the movements of the ultra-nationalist right, whether in France, Germany, Lithuania, or in more localised forms in Sweden, are seen as a serious threat to democracy and social advance. A new European left cannot be built, it is argued, unless this challenge is met, through the development of a multi-ethnic constitution for Europe.

MJR

cultural politics political cultures

One day conference at the University of Sussex
25 september 1998

What is the use of philosophy
  Feminism - an incomplete project
    Where is the contemporary public sphere
Does aesthetics offer freedom from capitalism
What does globalisation as a 'cultural' project look like
  Can national identity be reinvented by committee
      Can 'sub-politics' replace the political
    What is the truth of cultural studies
Is 'policy' the future of culture
Are voters rational subjects

?

The Anglo-American political studies tradition has been notoriously weak in its treatment of the cultural dimensions of politics. Meanwhile cultural studies at its most powerful has always been a mode of political engagement. Indeed it can be said to have failed when it does not succeed in offering cogent political analysis. Cultural theory is always political theory.

Cultural Studies' recent loss of direction can be attributed to its lack of relation to existing political projects in theory or practice, while the changes to political culture in recent decades - so often theorised under the confused heading of 'postmodernity' - can be understood as an erosion of the distinction between · 'Politics' and 'Culture'.

We invite papers addressing these problems, aiming to cross the boundaries between Cultural and Political Studies

For further information:

jeremy gilbert
Graduate research centre in culture
and communication
University of Sussex, Falmer, Brighton
BN1 9RJ

The radical centre

A politics without adversary

Chantal Mouffe

There is no 'third way'. The antagonisms of left/right politics are more relevant than ever.

Tales of the end of the right/left distinction have been with us for some time. Since the late 1980s this was accelerated by the collapse of communism - we have witnessed a clear move towards the centre in most socialist parties. But with New Labour in power a new twist has been added to this tale. We are told that a third way is now available: the 'radical centre'. After promoting the label of 'centre-left', Blair and his advisers now seem to prefer avoiding altogether any reference to the left. Since its victory, New Labour has begun to market itself as a radical movement, albeit of a new type. The novelty of this third way of 'radical centrism' supposedly consists in occupying a position which, by being located above left and right, manages to overcome the old antagonisms. Unlike the traditional centre, which lies in the middle of the spectrum between right and left, this is a centre that transcends the traditional left/right division by articulating themes and values from both sides in a new synthesis.

This radical centre, presented as the new model for progressive politics and

---

This article is dedicated to the memory of Ralph Miliband, who, on this issue, I hope would have agreed.

as the most promising alternative to old fashioned social democracy, draws on ideas developed by Anthony Giddens in his book *Beyond Left and Right*. Socialism, argues Giddens, was based on a 'cybernetic model' of social life which worked reasonably well in a world of 'simple modernisation', but which cannot work any more in a globalised, post-traditional social order characterised by the expansion of social reflexivity. In this brave new world of 'reflexive modernisation' we need a new type of radical politics, a 'generative' politics that allows people to make things happen and provides a framework for the life-political decisions of the individuals. Democracy should become 'dialogic' and, far from being limited to the political sphere, it should reach the various areas of personal life, aiming at a 'democracy of the emotions'. This new 'life'-politics overcomes, in his view, the traditional left/right divide since it draws from philosophical conservatism while preserving some of the core values usually associated with socialism.[1]

Alas, when examined more closely, stripped of its theoretical jargon and New Age rhetorical flourish, this radical centrism is oddly reminiscent of the strategy of 'triangulation' designed by Dick Morris for Bill Clinton's second-term campaign. In the case of Clinton there is no doubt that as an instrument of electoral propaganda it worked. By drawing on Republican ideas that resonated with voters - taxes, crime, welfare and the federal budget - and articulating them with leftist policies on abortion, education and the environment, Clinton managed to neutralise his adversaries and adroitly turn the tables in his favour. But who would want to call this radical politics?

L et me make clear at the outset that the problem I see in this notion of the radical centre is not its rejection of traditional left solutions. The critique of statism and productivism is far from new and many people who still identify with the left have long been aware of the shortcomings of traditional social democracy. The problem is not in the radical centre's embracing some conservative themes either. The postmodern critique of Enlightenment epistemology has for some time stressed the possibility of, and the need to, dissociate the left project from its rationalistic premises. Several attempts to reformulate the aims of the left in terms of 'radical and plural democracy' have pointed out how, by helping us to problematise the idea of

---

1. Anthony Giddens, *Beyond Left and Right*, Polity, Cambridge, 1994.

progress inherited from the Enlightenment, traditional conservative philosophers could contribute to the elaboration of a radical politics.

What is really the problem with the advocates of the 'radical centre' is, I believe, their claim that the left/right divide, an inheritance of 'simple modernisation', is no longer relevant in our era of 'reflexive modernisation'. By asserting that a radical politics today should transcend this divide and conceive democratic life as a dialogue, they imply that we live in a society which is no longer structured by social division. Relations of power and their constitutive role in society are disregarded; the conflicts that they entail are reduced to a simple competition between interests which can be harmonised through dialogue. This is the typical liberal perspective that envisages democracy as a struggle among elites, taking place in a neutral terrain, thereby making adversary forces invisible and reducing politics to an exchange of arguments and the negotiation of compromises. I want to argue that to present such a view of politics as 'radical' is disingenuous and that instead of being conducive to a greater democracy the radical centrism advocated by New Labour is in fact a renunciation of the basic tenet of radical politics: the definition of the adversary.

Conflict and modern democracy

One of the main problems nowadays is that the left's coming to terms with the importance of pluralism, and of liberal democratic institutions, has been accompanied by the mistaken belief that this means abandoning any attempt to offer an alternative to the present hegemonic order. Hence the sacralisation of consensus, the blurring of the left/right distinction and the present urge of many left parties to locate themselves at the centre. But this is to miss a crucial point, not only about the primary reality of strife in social life, but also about the integrative role which conflict plays in modern democracy. The specificity of modern democracy lies in the recognition and the legitimation of conflict and the refusal to suppress it through the imposition of an authoritarian order. Breaking with the symbolic representation of society as an organic body - which is characteristic of the holist mode of social organisation - a democratic society asserts pluralism and makes room for the expression of conflicting interests and values. A well-functioning democracy calls for a vibrant clash of democratic political positions. If this is missing there is always the danger that this democratic confrontation will be replaced by a confrontation between non-negotiable moral values or essentialist forms of identifications as is the case with identity politics. Too much emphasis on consensus, together with aversion towards confrontations, leads to apathy and to disaffection with political participation. Worse still, it may backfire with the result being an explosion of antagonisms unmanageable by the democratic process. This is why a vibrant democratic life requires real debate about possible alternatives. In other words while consensus is indeed necessary, it must be accompanied by dissent. There is no contradiction in saying that, as some would pretend. Consensus is needed on the institutions which are constitutive of democracy, but there will always be disagreement concerning the way social justice should be implemented in and through these institutions. In a pluralist democracy such disagreement should be considered legitimate and indeed welcome. We can agree on the importance of 'liberty and equality for all', while disagreeing sharply about their meaning and the way they should be implemented.

'The blurring of the left/right divide creates a democratic deficit and leads to the trivialisation of politics'

It is precisely this kind of disagreement which provides the stuff of democratic politics and it is what the struggle between left and right should be about. This is why, instead of giving up 'left' and 'right' as outdated terms, we should redefine them. When political frontiers become blurred, the dynamics of politics are obstructed and the constitution of distinctive political identities are hindered. Disaffection towards political parties sets in and in turn discourages participation in the political process. Alas, as we have begun to witness in many countries, the result is not a more mature, reconciled society, but the growth of other types of collective identities around religious, nationalist or ethnic forms of identifications. Antagonisms can take many forms and it is illusory to believe that they could ever be eliminated. This is why it is preferable to give them a political outlet within a pluralistic democratic system. The deplorable spectacle of the United States with the trivialisation of political stakes, reduced to the unmasking of sex scandals, provides a good example of the degeneration of the democratic public sphere. The focus on Clinton's sexual history is a direct consequence of this new kind of bland, homogenised political world resulting from the effects of triangulation. The development of a moralistic discourse and the obsessive unveiling of scandals, as well as the growth of various types of religious integrisms, are too often the consequence of the void created in political life by the absence of democratic forms of identifications informed by competing political values.

However the problem is not specific to the US. A look at other countries where, because of different traditions, the sexual card cannot be played in the same way as in the Anglo-American world shows that the crusade against corruption and shabby deals can play a similar role in replacing the missing political line of demarcation between adversaries. In other circumstances yet, the political frontier might be drawn around religious identities or around non-negotiable moral values, as in the case of abortion. But in all cases what this reveals is a democratic deficit created by the blurring of the left/right divide and the trivialisation of political discourse.

Another, perhaps more worrying, consequence of the same phenomenon is the increasing role played by extreme right-wing parties in many European countries. Indeed I submit that the rise of the far-right in France and Austria, for instance, should be understood in the context of the 'consensus at the centre' type of politics that has resulted in these particular countries from the growing ideological convergence between the main governing parties. This has allowed the National Front in France and the Freedom Party in Austria - the only parties to challenge the dominant consensus - to appear as anti-Establishment forces representing the will of the people. Thanks to a skilful populist rhetoric, they have been able to articulate many demands of the ordinary people, scorned as retrograde by the modernising elites, and they are trying to present themselves as the only guarantors of the sovereignty of the people. Such a situation, I believe, would not have been possible had more real political choices been available within the traditional democratic spectrum.

Politics and the political

Unfortunately, political theory, dominated as it is by a rationalistic and individualistic perspective, is completely unable to help us understand what is happening. Hence the urgency to develop an alternative approach. Against the views that envisage democracy as a 'dialogue', it is important to grasp the role of power relations in society and the ever present possibility of antagonism. In order to begin delineating a different conception of politics, one which acknowledges the centrality of antagonism, it may be useful to make a distinction between 'the political' and 'politics'. By 'the political', I mean the potential antagonism inherent in social relations, antagonism which can manifest itself in many different forms. 'Politics' refers to the ensemble of discourses, institutions and practices whose objective is to establish an order, to organise human co-existence in a context that is always conflictual because of the presence of 'the political'. Politics is concerned with the formation of an 'us' as opposed to a 'them'. It aims at the creation of unity in a context which is always one of conflict and diversity.

Envisaged from that angle, the novelty of democratic politics is not the overcoming of this us/them opposition, but the different way in which it is established. A pluralist democratic order supposes that the opponent is not considered as an enemy to be destroyed but as an adversary whose existence is legitimate and must be tolerated. We will fight against her ideas but we will not put into question her right to defend them. This category of the adversary does not eliminate antagonism, though, and it should be distinguished from the liberal notion of the competitor with which it is sometimes identified. An adversary, we could say, is an enemy with whom we have in common a shared adhesion to the ethico-political principles of democracy while disagreeing about their interpretation and implementation. However this disagreement is not one that could be resolved through rational argument because it involves power relations. Hence the antagonistic element in the relation.

To come to accept the position of the adversary is to undergo a radical change in political identity and it implies a shift in power relations. Certainly, compromises are possible and they are part of the process of politics, but these are only temporary respites in an ongoing confrontation in which it is impossible to satisfy everybody. There is a distinction which I take to be crucial for grasping the specificity of modern democratic politics: the distinction between antagonism and agonism. A relation of antagonism is one that takes place between enemies, while a relation of agonism takes place between adversaries. Against the two dominant models of democratic politics (the 'aggregative' one that reduces politics to the negotiation of interests and the 'deliberative' or 'dialogic' one which believes that decisions on matters of common concern should result from the free and unconstrained public deliberation of all) I envisage democratic politics as a form of 'agonistic pluralism'. This is a way to envisage democracy which, starting with the recognition of power relations and the conflicts that they entail, stresses that in modern democratic politics the crucial problem is how to transform antagonism into agonism. In other words, the aim of democratic institutions from this perspective is not to establish a rational consensus in the public sphere; it is to provide democratic channels of expression for the forms of conflicts considered as legitimate.

Envisaging modern democracy as a form of agonistic pluralism has very important consequences for politics. Once it is acknowledged that this type of agonistic confrontation is what is specific to a pluralist democracy, we can understand why such a democracy requires the creation of collective identities around clearly differentiated positions, as well as the possibility to choose between real alternatives. This is precisely the function of the left/right distinction. The left/right opposition is the mean through which legitimate conflict is given form and institutionalised. If this framework does not exist or is weakened, the process of transformation of antagonism into agonism is hindered and this can have dire consequences for democracy. This is why discourses about the 'end of politics' and the irrelevance of the left/right distinction should not be cause for celebration, but for concern. The traditional framework of left and right is in serious need of overhauling and it is not a question of merely reasserting the old slogans and the dogmatic certainties. However it would be a mistake to believe that such a distinction could be transcended and that a radical politics could exist without defining an adversary.

Which globalisation?
Those who argue for the need to go beyond right and left affirm that in the type of globalised, reflexive society in which we live, neither conservatism nor socialism can provide adequate solutions. No doubt this is the case. Moreover it is true that in political practice the categories of left and right have become increasingly blurred. But to infer from that empirical fact a thesis concerning the necessary irrelevance of such a distinction, or to make a value judgement about the desirability of its disappearance, is another matter. This might make sense from the perspective of a liberal approach unable to recognise the constitutive role of relations of power and the ineradicability of antagonism; but for those who aim at formulating a progressive politics it is necessary to acknowledge the dimension of what I have called 'the political' and the impossibility of a reconciled society. Our task should be to redefine the left in

order to re-activate the democratic struggle, not to proclaim its obsolescence. There is in advanced democratic societies an urgent need to re-establish the centrality of politics and this requires drawing new political frontiers capable of giving a real impulse to democracy. One of the crucial stakes for left democratic politics is to begin providing an alternative to neo-liberalism. It is the current unchallenged hegemony of the neo-liberal discourse which explains why the left is without any credible project. Paradoxically, while increasingly victorious politically - since it is in power in many European countries - the left is still thoroughly out-manouvered ideologically. This is why it is unable to take the intellectual initiative. Instead of trying to build a new hegemony, it has capitulated to the neo-liberal one. Witness the desperate strategy of 'triangulation' whose outcome is the 'Thatcherism with a human face' trademark of New Labour.

Globalisation is the usual justification given for the 'there is no alternative' dogma. Indeed, the argument most often rehearsed against redistributive-type social-democratic policies is that the tight fiscal restraints faced by the government are the only realistic possibility in a world where voters refuse to pay more taxes and where global markets would not allow any deviation from neo-liberal orthodoxy. This kind of argument takes for granted the ideological terrain which has been established as a result of years of neo-liberal hegemony and transforms what is a conjunctural state of affairs into an historical necessity. Here, as in many other cases, the mantra of globalisation is invoked to justify the status-quo and reinforce the power of big transnational corporations.[2]

When it is presented as driven exclusively by the information revolution, globalisation becomes detached from its political dimension and appears as a fate to which we all have to submit. This is precisely where our critique should begin. Scrutinising this conception, André Gorz has recently argued that, instead of being seen as the necessary consequence of a technological revolution, the process of globalisation must be understood as a move by capital to provide what was a fundamentally political answer to the 'crisis of governability' of the 1970s.[3] In his view, the crisis of the fordist model of development led to a divorce

---

2. For a similar argument see the editorial of *Soundings* No 7, *States of Africa* by Doreeen Massey.
3. André Gorz, *Misères du present, Richesse du ible*, Galilée, Paris 1997.

between the interests of capital and those of the nation states. The space of politics became dissociated from the space of the economy. This phenomenon of globalisation was made possible by new forms of technology. But this technological revolution required for its implementation a profound transformation in the relations of power among social groups and between capitalist corporations and the state. The political move was the crucial one. The result is that today corporations have gained a sort of extra-territoriality. They have managed to emancipate themselves from political power and to appear the real locus of sovereignty. No wonder the resources needed to finance the welfare state are diminishing since the states are unable to tax the transnational corporations.

By unveiling the strategies of power which have informed the process of globalisation, Gorz's approach allows us to see the possibility for a counter-strategy. Of course it is vain to simply attempt to resist globalisation from the context of the nation state. It is only by opposing the power of transnational capital - another globalisation, informed by a different political project - that we could have a chance to resist successfully neo-liberalism and to install a new hegemony. However such a counter-hegemonic strategy is precisely what is precluded by the very idea of a radical centrism which denies the existence of antagonisms and the need for political frontiers. To believe that one can accommodate the aims of the big corporations with those of the weaker sectors of society is already to have capitulated to their power. It is to have accepted their globalisation as the only possible one and to act within the constraints that capital is imposing on national governments. The adherents of such a view see politics as a game where potentially the demands of all could be met without anybody having to lose. For New Labour there is of course neither enemy nor adversary. For them everybody or organisation are part of 'the people'. The interests of Murdoch, Formula One, or the rich transnational corporations, can be happily reconciled with those of the unemployed, single mothers and the disabled. Social cohesion is to be secured not through equality and solidarity but through strong families and shared moral values.

A new left-wing project

Radical politics cannot be located at the centre because to be radical - as Margaret Thatcher, contrary to Tony Blair, very well knew - is to aim at a profound transformation of power relations. This cannot be done without drawing political frontiers and defining an adversary or even an enemy. Of course a radical project cannot be successful without winning over many of those who are located at the centre. All significant victories of the left have been the result of an alliance of important sectors of the middle classes, whose interests have been articulated, and those of the popular sectors. Today more than ever such an alliance is vital for the formulation of a radical project. But this does not mean that such an alliance requires taking the middle ground and trying to establish a compromise between neo-liberalism and the groups that it oppresses. There are many issues concerning the provision of decent public services and the creation of good conditions of life on which a broad alliance could be established. However this cannot take place without the elaboration of new hegemonic project that would put again on the agenda the struggle for equality which has been discarded by the advocates of neo-liberalism.

Perhaps the clearest sign of New Labour's renunciation of its left identity is that is has abandoned such a struggle for equality. Under the pretence of formulating a modern, post-social democratic conception of equality, Blairites have eschewed the language of redistribution in order to speak exclusively in terms of inclusion and exclusion. As if the very condition for inclusion of the excluded were not a drastic redistribution and a correction of the profound inequalities which the neo-liberal long decade has brought about.

The current avoidance by New Labour of the theme of equality, and its increasing acceptance of inequalities, is very symptomatic indeed. As Norberto Bobbio recently reminded us, it is the idea of equality which provides the backbone of the left vision while the right has always defended diverse forms of inequality.[4] The fact that a certain type of egalitarian ideology has been used to justify totalitarian forms of politics in no way forces us to relinquish the struggle for equality. What a left-wing project today requires is to envisage this struggle for equality in a way that takes account of the multiplicity of social relations in which inequality needs to be challenged. This will of course require a critique of the shortcomings of traditional social democracy. If Thatcherism was successful it is in part because it was able to re-articulate in its favour the popular resentment against those shortcomings. I have no problem therefore with the

---

4.   Norberto Bobbio, *Left and Right*, Polity, Cambridge, 1996.

idea of a 'post-social democratic politics', on condition that this does not mean regressing behind social democracy to some pre-social democratic liberal view. Yet this type of regression appears to be precisely the kind of move that is behind the logic of the welfare-to-work policies advocated by Blairites.

John Gray, another of Blair's advisers, celebrates New Labour for having abandoned a redistributive, social democratic idea of justice but worries that they have not put anything in its place. He urges them to re-invent liberal Britain by embracing the New Liberalism advocated in the early decades of this century by L.T. Hobhouse and T.H. Green. According to such a liberalism, says Gray, economic inequalities were not unfair and the important issue was to reconcile the demands of individual choice with the needs for social cohesion.[5]

While agreeing with Gray in his critique of 'egalitarianism', I believe that he establishes a false dichotomy between equality and individual freedom. To be sure there will always be a tension between those values and it is unrealistic to believe that they could be perfectly reconciled, but it does not mean that they are incompatible and that we have to discard one in pursuit of the other. For those who still identify with the left there are ways to envisage a social justice which is committed to both pluralism and equality. Several theorists have been concerned with developing such a perspective. For instance in *Spheres of Justice*, Michael Walzer elaborates a conception which he calls 'complex equality'.[6] He argues that if one wants to make equality a central objective of a politics that also respects liberty it is necessary to abandon the idea of 'simple equality' which tends to render people as equal as possible in all areas. Equality in his view is a complex relationship between persons mediated by a series of social goods; it does not consist in an identity of possession. According to the complex view of equality that he advocates, social goods should be distributed, not in a uniform manner but in terms of a diversity of criteria which reflect the diversity of those social goods and the meaning attached to them. The important thing, he argues, is not to violate the principles of distribution proper to each sphere. One needs to preclude success in one sphere implying the possibility of exercising preponderance in others, as is now the case with wealth. It is essential that no social good be used as the means of

---

5. John Gray, 'Goodbye to Rawls', *Prospect*, November 1997.
6. Michael Walzer, *Spheres of Justice*, Basic Books, New York, 1983.

domination and that concentration of political power, wealth, honour and offices in the same hands should be avoided. Thinking along those lines would allow us to envisage the struggle against inequality in a way that would respect and deepen pluralism instead of stifling individual freedom.

The main problem that a post-social democratic vision informed by a view of complex equality will have to tackle, a problem of which the welfare-to-work policies of New Labour seem to be unaware, is the crucial transformation with which our societies are confronted: the crisis of work and the exhaustion of the wage society. In this area, more than any other perhaps, it is evident that we have entered a quite different world in which neither laissez-faire liberalism nor Keynesianism will be able to provide a solution. The problem of unemployment calls for new radical thinking. Without a realisation that there will be no return to full employment (if that ever existed) and that a new model of economic development is urgently needed, no alternative to neo-liberalism will ever take off. The Americanisation of Europe will proceed under the liberal motto of 'flexibilisation'.

A truly radical project needs to start by acknowledging that, as a consequence of the information revolution, there is a growing dissociation between the production of wealth and the quantity of work needed to produce it. Without a drastic redistribution in the average effective duration of work, society will become increasingly polarised between those who work in stable, regular jobs and the rest who are either unemployed or have part-time, precarious and unprotected jobs. Jointly with such a redistribution, a plural economy should be developed where the associative sector would play an important role alongside the market and the state sector. Many activities, of crucial social utility but discarded by the logic of the market, could, through public financing, be carried out in this solidaristic economy. There is however a third element to take into account. Indeed the condition for the success of such initiatives is the implementation of some form of citizen's income that would guarantee a decent minimum for everybody. This is an idea that has recently been gaining an increasing number of supporters who argue that the reform of the welfare state would be better approached by envisaging the different modalities of such an income than by replacing it by workfare.

Implemented together these measures could create the basis for a post-social democratic answer to neo-liberalism. Of course such an answer could only be carried out successfully in a European context and this is why a left-wing project today could only be a European one. In this time of globalisation the taming of capitalism cannot be realised at the level of the nation state. Only within the context of an integrated Europe, in which the different states would unite their forces, could the attempt to make finance capital more accountable succeed. If, instead of competing among themselves in order to establish the more attractive deals for transnational corporations, the different European states would agree on common policies, another type of globalisation could be possible. That the traditional conceptions of both the left and the right are inadequate for the problems that we are facing at the eve of the new millennium is something that I readily accept, but to believe that the antagonisms that those categories evoke have disappeared in our globalised world is to fall prey to the hegemonic neo-liberal discourse of the end of politics. Far from having lost their relevance, the stakes to which the left and the right allude are more pertinent than ever.

A last word on New Labour. Given its mistaken conception of the democratic process, we should not be surprised at the fact that it is unable to accept the expression of dissent in its midst. Its authoritarianism chimes with its conception of a consensual politics of dialogue from which strife has been eliminated. Such a conception cannot make room for the conflict inherent in social life. As I have tried to show, the radical centre is unable to acknowledge the importance of an agonistic confrontation. Every expression of dissent is therefore seen as the manifestation of an antagonism that will threaten Labour's existence. However this politics without an adversary is a flawed conception. By wanting to include everybody in 'the people', and have the powerful cohabit with the oppressed, New Labour perpetuates the continued subordination of the very people that it was meant to defend and represent. In the end it cannot do without adversaries, except that since it cannot see them in Murdoch and his likes, it must resort to the part of 'the people' that resists being 'dialogically' domesticated: 'Old Labour', which is depicted as the enemy. Alas politics always calls for decision. When the stakes are on the table, one needs to choose one's camp, there is no 'third way'. The centre - radical or not - has to take sides. We can only hope that New Labour will not learn that lesson too late.

New labour, new monetarism

Philip Arestis and Malcolm Sawyer

New Labour's economic policies share much in common with old-fashioned monetarism, particularly in their narrow focus on interest rates as an instrument of policy.

The notion that economic policy follows a coherent strategy drawn from a clear economic analysis of capitalist economies would be laughable. But it is often possible to discern some general tendencies and to see the influence of economic ideas on economic policy. We would not go as far as Keynes when he wrote that:

> the ideas of economists and political philosophers, both when they are right and when they are wrong, are more powerful than is commonly understood. Indeed the world is ruled by little else. Practical men, who believe themselves to be quite exempt from any intellectual influences, are usually the slaves of some defunct economists. Madmen in authority, who hear voices in the air, are distilling their frenzy from some academic scribbler of a few years back.[1]

Indeed, we would acknowledge that a politician's adoption of ideas from economists can arise from those ideas leading to policy conclusions which the politician wanted to follow for other reasons. The early years of the Thatcher government illustrate the influence of economic ideas, usually described as monetarism, and how the interpretation of those ideas could be used to promote

---

1. See J.M. Keynes, *The General Theory of Employment, Interest and Money*, Macmillan, London 1936, p383.

policies which the government wished to pursue anyway. At the danger of giving the current government's economic policies more coherence than they deserve, we argue that there is a set of ideas that lie at the heart of the economic policies of New Labour. Since these ideas have a clear resonance with those associated with monetarism, we designate them as the 'new monetarism', and we refer to those which influenced the Thatcher government as 'old monetarism'.

We begin by describing the monetarism of the 1980s, which we label as 'old monetarism', and note the failures of simple monetarism through problems with control of the stock of money. But, we argue, 'old monetarism' also involved privileging the financial sector over the productive sector, and viewed economic difficulties as arising from government intervention in the labour market. We proceed by describing a 'new monetarism' which we see as central to the economic policies of New Labour. This 'new monetarism' also privileges finance and seeks to change the labour market; the implicit assumption appears to be that the levels of investment and of aggregate demand take care of themselves.

Old monetarism

Monetarism was often summarised in the phrase 'money matters', in supposed contrast to Keynesianism, which was accused of neglecting the role of money. This was not only an inaccurate interpretation of Keynesianism but overstates monetarism. It could be more accurately characterised by saying that money matters for the control of inflation but does not matter a jot for unemployment. The main architect of monetarism, Milton Friedman, advocated the adoption of a policy rule that the stock of money should increase by a predetermined amount: he argued that a growth in the money stock of say 5 per cent per annum in the context of real growth of 3 per cent per annum would generate inflation of 2 per cent per annum.[2] It was also argued that if people know that the money stock will grow at 5 per cent with the implication of 2 per cent inflation, they will act accordingly: for example, wages will be set with the expectation of 2 per cent inflation. In an open economy, the exchange rate will reflect differences between inflation in the countries concerned.

---

2. Milton Friedman's evidence to the Treasury and Civil Service Committee provides a very good summary of his ideas. See Friedman, *Memoranda on Monetary Policy*, Treasury and Civil Service Committee, HC 720-11, July 1980.

The policy then adopted in both the United Kingdom and the United States involved the setting of targets for the growth of the money stock (associated with the advent of the Thatcher and Reagan governments respectively, but with precedents in the previous Callaghan and Carter administrations). In both cases, the attempts at tight money drove up interest rates, after a decade of low real interest rates, for although nominal interest rates had been high during the 1970s those rates were often below the rate of inflation, with negative real rates of interest. This set the stage for an era of much higher interest rates than had previously been experienced: real rates of interest have typically been around 5 per cent per annum since 1980, compared with historic averages of 2 to 3 per cent per annum. The recessions of the early 1980s in the UK and in the USA did much to undermine the monetarist approach since that theory did not indicate that monetary deflation would involve major reductions in output and employment.

Simple monetarism, by which we mean control of the money supply to set the rate of inflation, soon collapsed. At this level, the causes of the collapse are straightforward. There were evident difficulties in controlling the money supply, and the targets for monetary growth were persistently missed. In Table 1 we cite targets and outcomes for the UK money stock (the sterling M3 definition) and for the Public Sector Borrowing Requirement (PSBR) as set in the period 1980-1985, under the Medium Term Financial Strategy. The assumption which was made by monetarists was that some part of the PSBR would be financed by the government printing money (technically MO, that is cash and reserves with the Bank of England) and this would then lead to an expansion in the broader definitions of money such as sterling M3 (broadly deposits with banks). It is clear from this table that over the period in question, money supply targets were always missed.[3] The PSBR targets were also missed with the exception of two cases, but then only after the relevant targets were raised subsequently. That was in 1981/82 and 1982/83, but witness the persistent raising of the target in the latter period.

Fixing PSBR to hit a certain target for the money supply is an extremely

---

3. In October 1985 the 1985/86 target for sterling M3 was suspended and finally abandoned in the budget of 1987. The suspended 1985/86 target was set at 5-9 per cent with an out-turn of 14.4 per cent. In the 1986 Budget the target for 1986/87 was set at 11-15 per cent which was significantly overshot yet again.

difficult, if not impossible, task. And so it proved to be. Whilst Milton Friedman could blame traitors in the Bank of England (as in Friedman 1980), that experience only served to confirm that in a sophisticated financial system where

Table 1: Monetary targets and the outturns

	Year target imposed and outturn	1980/81	1981/82	1982/83	1983/84	1984/85
Growth of Money Supply (% change)	March 1980	7 - 11	6 - 10	5 - 9	4 - 8	
	March 1981		6 - 10	5 - 9	4 - 8	
	March 1982			8 - 12	7 - 11	6 - 10
	March 1983				7 - 11	6 - 10
	March 1984					6 - 10
	Outturn	18.9	14.8	12.3	11.2	12.0
Public Sector Borrowing Requirement as % of GDP at market prices	March 1980	3.75	3	2.25	1.5	
	March 1981		4.25	3.25	2.0	
	March 1982			3.5	2.75	
	March 1983				2.75	
	March 1984					2.25
	Outturn	5.75	3.49	3.37	3.25	3.25

Source: *Economic Trends*, June 1985

money is created through the credit process by banks, it is well nigh impossible to control the stock of money. There has always been a paradox at the heart of monetarism, namely that monetarists argued that markets should not be controlled in any way, but the money stock created in the financial markets could and should be controlled. During the 1970s, monetarists had made much of a link between changes in the stock of money and the rate of inflation, operating with roughly a two year lag: hence control the stock of money now, so to be able to influence inflation two years hence. But the growth of the money stock indicated in Table 1 was much greater than that of the rate of inflation.

Other countries shared the British experience. In the case of Germany, the Bundesbank has failed to meet the monetary target on 10 occasions in the 21 years from 1975 to 1995 (inclusive).[4] Where does the reputation of the Bundesbank come from? In the case of the USA, monetary targets were missed there too (with the exception of the years 1981 and 1984) and in 1986 they were suspended, never to appear again.[5]

Another and more enduring aspect of monetarism is the view that unemployment would move to its 'natural level' (the 'natural rate of unemployment'). This is obviously a significant use of words with clear overtones of inevitability about unemployment. But the 'natural' rate of unemployment would (in theory) constitute full employment with a balance between the demand for and supply of labour if the labour market were akin to the perfectly competitive model. In lay person's terms, this would be a labour market in which wages and employment could change quickly as the composition of demand varied: what some would call a flexible labour market, and what others would see as an insecure spot market for labour. This 'flexible' competitive labour market could be achieved if 'imperfections' were removed. These 'imperfections' were associated with features such as trade union power, minimum wages imposed by Wage Councils, unemployment benefits, etc. It was precisely legislation to remove these 'imperfections' which formed a major part of the Thatcher agenda.

---

4. Information taken from the Annual Report of the Bundesbank, 1995, p77.
5. For more details of the USA experience see, Arestis. P and M. Marshall, 'The New Right and the US economy in the 1980s: An assessment of the economic record of the Reagan administration', *International Review of Applied Economics*, Vol 4, No 1, 1990, pp52-54.

Thus monetarism encapsulated the view that unemployment arose essentially from constraints on the flexible functioning of the labour market, constraints which could be repaired through legislation which reduced the power of trade unions and the influence of the state. This represented a major shift from previous perceptions. No longer was unemployment attributed to inadequate aggregate demand which could be addressed through fiscal and monetary expansion. The Conservative government declared in 1985 that the one thing clearly not responsible for unemployment is a lack of demand and that the biggest single cause of our high unemployment is the failure of our jobs market, the weak link in our economy.[6] Nor was unemployment and sluggish growth to be placed at the door of industry because of a failure to invest and to achieve international competitiveness. Monetarism represented the triumph of the market over the state, in the sense that it viewed failures of the labour market (to generate full employment) as due to external government interventions such as unemployment benefits, minimum wage legislation etc, and that it accepted that the product market and private industry operated in an efficient manner.

Related to this aspect, there is the notion of the 'flexibility' of labour markets which is often used to explain the lower recorded unemployment rate in the UK (around 7 per cent) as compared with the higher rates (22 per cent in the case of Spain) in much of the rest of the European Union. The point is highlighted in Table 2 where standardised unemployment rates are given for recent years. Whilst it is true that the UK unemployment rate has been decreasing especially since 1993 (which can be explained by the forced devaluation of the pound in 1992), other countries in the EU (Austria, Denmark, Luxembourg, The Netherlands and Portugal) have been doing much better than the UK. But even for the other EU countries which have been experiencing significantly higher unemployment rates than the UK, this can be explained by their efforts to meet the stringent Maastricht criteria (Belgium, Finland, France, Germany, Greece, Italy, Ireland, Spain and Sweden). If we take into account countries outside the EU, the picture is pretty much the same. Norway and Australia, where allegedly

---

6. See, Department of Employment, *Employment: The Challenge for the Nation*, Cmnd. 9774, HMSO, London 1985. This document went on to argue that since 1979 Britain has begun a revolution in education and training and that the Government can help to improve the labour market by encouraging better training, more flexibility and fewer barriers of regulation and cost, pp15-23.

Table 2 Standardised unemployment rates

EU Countries	1992	1993	1994	1995	1996	1997
Austria	3.6	4.2	3.8	3.9	4.4	6.6
Belgium	7.3	8.9	10.0	9.9	9.8	9.7
Denmark	9.2	10.1	8.2	7.2	6.9	6.4
Finland	13.0	17.7	17.4	16.2	15.3	15.3
France	10.4	11.7	12.3	11.7	12.4	12.6
Germany	6.6	7.9	8.4	8.2	8.9	9.5
Greece	7.9	8.6	8.9	9.7	9.8	10.0
Ireland	15.1	15.6	14.3	12.3	11.8	10.8
Italy	9.0	10.3	11.4	11.9	12.0	12.2
Luxembourg	2.1	2.7	3.2	2.9	3.3	3.7
Netherlands	5.6	6.6	7.1	6.9	6.3	5.6
Portugal	4.2	5.7	7.0	7.3	7.3	6.2
Spain	18.5	22.8	24.1	22.9	22.1	20.9
Sweden	5.6	9.5	9.8	9.2	10.0	10.7
UK	10.1	10.4	9.6	8.8	8.2	7.4
Average for EU countries	8.6	10.2	10.4	9.9	9.9	10.0
Non EU countries						
Australia	10.7	11.0	9.8	8.6	8.6	8.7
Canada	11.3	11.2	10.4	9.5	9.7	9.5
Japan	2.2	2.5	2.9	3.1	3.4	3.4
Norway	5.9	6.1	5.5	5.0	4.9	4.2
USA	7.5	6.9	6.1	5.6	5.4	5.2
Average for non-EU countries	7.5	7.5	6.9	6.4	6.4	6.2

Source: *OECD Economic Outlook*; Labour Market Trends and Ministry of National Economy

Table 3 Standardised employment figures: percentage changes from previous period

	1992	1993	1994	1995	1996*	1997*
EU COUNTRIES						
Austria	1.5	- 0.3	0.2	- 0.4	-0.7	-0.2
Belgium	- 0.4	- 1.1	- 0.7	0.4	-0.1	0.5
Denmark	- 0.6	- 1.0	- 0.6	1.6	1.0	1.0
Finland	- 7.1	- 6.1	- 0.8	2.2	1.1	1.5
France	- 0.6	- 1.2	0.1	0.9	0.0	0.3
Germany	- 1.8	- 1.7	- 0.7	- 0.3	-0.9	0.2
Greece	1.5	0.9	1.9	0.9	0.8	0.9
Ireland	0.4	1.8	3.5	4.0	3.2	2.0
Italy	- 0.9	- 2.5	- 1.7	- 0.6	0.4	0.1
Luxembourg	2.5	1.8	2.3	2.5	2.3	2.6
Netherlands	1.6	0.7	-0.1	2.4	1.9	1.8
Portugal	- 6.4	- 2.0	-0.1	-0.6	0.4	0.4
Spain	- 1.9	- 4.3	-0.9	1.7	1.3	1.6
Sweden	- 4.3	- 5.8	-0.9	1.6	-0.5	0.5
UK	- 2.4	- 0.8	0.7	0.6	0.2	0.8
Average for EU Countries	- 1.3	-0.7	0.0	1.0	0.7	0.9
NON-EU COUNTRIES						
Australia	- 0.7	0.4	3.1	4.1	1.3	1.9
Canada	- 0.6	1.4	2.1	1.6	1.4	1.9
Japan	1.1	0.2	0.1	0.1	0.6	1.1
Norway	- 0.3	0.0	1.5	2.0	2.4	1.3
USA	0.7	1.5	2.3	1.6	1.4	1.2
Average for Non-EUCountries	- 0.04	0.7	1.8	1.9	1.4	1.5

Source: *OECD Economic Outlook*, 1997
* These are estimates and projections.

inflexible labour markets exist, have been doing much better than the UK. At the same time Canada, with an economy comparable to that of the UK, has been doing worse than the UK. Japan and the USA have had mixed experiences, where the USA has been doing rather better recently, but Japan's unemployment rates have been consistently lower than the USA's.

The picture is too mixed to arrive at any generalised conclusions. Furthermore, if employment rates were used, the picture is not as markedly different amongst the EU countries, as shown in Table 3. With the exceptions of Luxembourg and The Netherlands, the rest of the EU tends to have more or less the same pattern. The comparison with the non-EU countries is still roughly similar to the unemployment case. Countries outside the EU have been doing a great deal better than the countries within it, and consistently so throughout the period since 1992.

Tobin distinguishes between Monetarism Mark 1 (broadly associated with Milton Friedman) and Monetarism Mark 2 (associated with another Nobel Prize winner, Robert Lucas).[7] The particular 'contribution' of Lucas which is relevant to this discussion is the stress on 'rational expectations': the idea that when people form a view about the future, they do so using all the information at their disposal and the 'true model' of how the economy works (which is well known and understood by economic agents), and this view of the future is broadly accurate and does not contain any systematic errors. It is difficult to understate the impact of this idea on economic thinking, and indirectly on economic policy. When those working in the market are assumed as knowledgeable as they were by 'rational expectations', it carries a strong presumption that the 'market knows best'. Since the markets which respond most quickly and where prices change on a minute to minute basis are the financial markets, the assumption of 'rational expectations' points to the wisdom of the financial markets. This same idea also led to the notion that financial markets were 'efficient', and that share prices, exchange rates, etc., reflected an accurate assessment of the prospects for a company (in the case of share prices) and for an economy (in the case of exchange rates).[8] Furthermore, an economic

---

7. J.Tobin, 'The Monetarist counter-revolution today – an appraisal', *Economic Journal*, Vol 91, 1981, pp29-42.
8. It is difficult to write this with a straight face as it is being drafted after a week which saw the Hong Kong stock market drop by 15 per cent one day, then rise by 15 per cent the next!

policy could only be implemented if the financial markets deemed it to be credible: if the policy was not credible, then financial markets would indicate as much (e.g. by the exchange rate falling). What matters then is not so much whether a policy is credible, but whether the financial markets believe it to be so. It also provides a great get-out clause for policy-makers: a policy of increased public expenditure cannot be undertaken because the financial markets would deem it incredible and unsustainable. In addition, monetarism also represented the acceptance of the power and wisdom of the financial markets, especially as monetarism developed and incorporated 'rational expectations'. The financial markets had to be convinced that the government wished to reduce inflation, and this could be brought about through announcement of money supply targets.

New monetarism

Under the monetarism of the 1980s (which we will now refer to as 'old monetarism'), the monetary policy was to control the growth of the stock of money through monetary targets (and the use of interest rates to help reach those targets) with the intention that the growth of money stock would determine the rate of inflation. 'New monetarism' is rather similar: the inflation rate target is set (currently at 2.5 per cent), and the operationally independent Bank of England is given the responsibility to manipulate interest rates to achieve that inflationary target. The mechanism by which that is to happen is never made clear.[9] However (at least) three possible routes can be identified. The first route is that the interest rate rise is expected to lower aggregate demand, leading to lower (than otherwise) output, and the lower demand places downward pressure on inflation. An interest rate hike would be predicted to have some adverse effect on investment, though it may be questioned whether a small percentage change has any marked effect. In so far as this sub route is operable, future productive capacity is lower and the ability of the economy to support employment reduced. The effects of interest rates on savings is usually seen to be ambiguous. But dissavings by households (that is the financing of expenditure through debt) is likely to be affected, and consumer expenditure reduced accordingly. A more significant sub route may be the 'income effect', that is

---

9. The Treasury Select Committee requested in November 1997 that the Bank of England makes its views of the monetary transmission mechanism known.

higher interest rates raise mortgage payments (on variable interest rates), reducing disposable income and then consumer expenditure. This is offset by the increased income of the interest recipients (wealth holders), but it is usually presumed that the net effect on consumer expenditure is negative. A problem with this channel is that if it is assumed that a higher interest rate lowers nominal expenditure, then the question arises of how the nominal expenditure fall splits between prices and real output.

The second route is a monetary one. A higher base rate leads to generally higher interest rates including those on loans; this would lower the demand for loans with fewer loans being granted and less money created. As a consequence, the money stock is lower than it would have been. A monetarist story can then be added to this: the lower money stock leads to a lower (than otherwise) price level, and this lower price level means a lower rate of inflation. But this would presume that the lower money stock somehow generates a lower demand for money. The monetarist view is that the lower stock (supply) forces a lower demand: but the post-Keynesian view would be rather different, namely that the stock would adjust to the demand. Indeed, if the inflation rate is not a monetary phenomenon - say it is determined by a process of adding a mark-up on costs - then this process would be highly deflationary with considerable decreases in output and thus increases in unemployment.

The third route could be labelled the New Zealand disease, namely that the pursuit of an inflation target through interest rate policy leads to higher interest rates which drive up the exchange rate. This higher exchange rate tends to reduce inflation as the price (in the domestic currency) of imports fall. The fall in import prices may not fully reflect the rise in the exchange rate: that would depend on the strategy of the importers. But the exchange rate rise causes difficulties for exporters: how much difficulty depends on their market power and how far they can raise prices in the foreign currency and preserve prices in the domestic currency. The prices of non-traded goods and services are not directly influenced by this rise in the exchange rate, and domestic factors largely govern the rate of increase of prices of non-traded goods and services. The rate of inflation is essentially a weighted average of the inflation rate on traded goods (held down by the exchange rate rise) and the rate on non-traded goods. There is a strong possibility that the price of traded goods falls relative to the price of non-traded goods. This route has been labelled the New Zealand disease because the independence of the New Zealand Central Bank appears to have precisely these effects. In the past few years in New Zealand, the overall rate of inflation has been around 2 per cent per annum, whilst the rate for tradable goods has been less than 1 per cent, and that for non-tradable around 4 per cent. From 1992 onwards, the real exchange rate (as well as the nominal exchange rate) has been on an upward trajectory and has appreciated by around 30 per cent. This third route can only work if the exchange rate rises: the other side of that coin is that the exchange rates of other countries fall. If other countries then join in, raising interest rates to stem the fall in their exchange rate (and perhaps in the pursuit of inflation targets), the outcome is competitive revaluation of the exchange rate and competitive interest rate hikes.

The Labour Party in opposition decried what they termed the 'one club' approach, in which interest rates were the only policy instrument being used to guide the economy. And yet this seems to be what is now happening again. Interest rates are being used to guide the economy, responding to perceptions of an overheating economy. Fiscal policy is now heavily constrained, and has been virtually ruled out for purposes of guiding the

> 'The use of fiscal policy to regulate aggregate demand has been given up completely'

economy, throwing the weight for that guidance on to interest rates. The scope available for fiscal policy is limited through adherence to the Maastricht criteria (limiting the budget deficit to 3 per cent of GDP) and through pronouncements in favour of balanced budgets, the so-called 'golden rule' of public finance (that government should only borrow to meet capital expenditure) and concerns over the size of debt and of interest payments (which are exacerbated by the high interest rate policy).[10] Further, public expenditure plans are locked into those decreed by the previous government, and tax rises are ruled out politically. Thus the use of fiscal policy to regulate aggregate demand in the economy is given up completely. Furthermore, under 'old monetarism', the government was to act under monetary targets

---

10. Under this rule, borrowing to finance the purchase of military equipment is permissible as it counts as capital expenditure; borrowing to finance the employment of teachers, health service workers or to pay disability benefits (and many other measures) is not.

to inform the financial markets of their intentions on inflation. Under 'new monetarism', the government gives the Bank of England operational independence over the setting of interest rates with the sole objective of meeting a target rate of inflation to assure the financial markets. 'New monetarism' also involves an acceptance of the power and wisdom of the financial markets. In short, fiscal policy is completely subordinated to monetary policy, and this can at most only regulate the inflation rate. Inflation is prioritised over improving the industrial base, promotion of competitiveness, and employment. No regard is paid to ensuring that there is adequate demand in the economy, and fiscal policy is effectively renounced.

It is notable that, in their manifesto for the 1997 election, the Labour Party made no proposals for the control of inflation other than to set a target of 2.5 per cent or less. This was followed by the reform of the Bank of England with operational independence being granted in the very early stages of the Labour government; the clear implication being that granting independence to the Bank was a signal that inflation can be controlled through manipulation of the interest rate. It is a rather strange feature of current political debate that inflation is seen as 'evil' and yet no attention is given to how inflation can be contained.[11] Two interpretations come to mind. The first is the acceptance that unemployment, engineered through higher interest rates, can be used to contain inflation. We have doubts on both the morality and the effectiveness of such an approach. But in the infamous words of Norman Lamont, high unemployment is seen as 'a price worth paying' for low inflation. The second is to argue that inflation within the industrialised world remains low. A combination of globalisation, weakened trade unions, and lowered inflationary expectations after nearly twenty years of anti-inflationary policies, would ensure that inflation does not re-emerge as a serious problem, which some have described as the 'death of inflation'. If that is the case, then there is little need to pay any regard to inflation as a problem, and it would be time to turn to the many other problems which beset the economy.

'Old monetarism' invoked the 'natural rate of unemployment'. 'New monetarism' draws on a similar concept in the form of the Non-Accelerating Inflation Rate of Unemployment, affectionately known as the NAIRU. The

---

11. Tony Blair, *The Mais Lecture*, text of lecture delivered 22 May 1995.

NAIRU is somewhat mislabelled since it involves a non-rising rather than non-accelerating rate of inflation. The idea is simply that a level of unemployment below the NAIRU would involve rising inflation: wages would tend to rise faster than prices, which in turn would respond by rising even faster. Unemployment above the NAIRU would lead to falling inflation. For the believers in the NAIRU, it can be calculated from the estimation of equations describing wage and price formation, with some recent estimates putting it in the range 5 to 7 per cent. Grieve Smith summarises the position accurately when he writes that 'at present the objective implicit in the inflation target is to prevent unemployment falling below a certain minimum level', where that minimum level is well above the level of unemployment which would correspond to full employment.[12] A particularly pernicious aspect of the NAIRU is that a belief in its existence means that unemployment falling below that level is taken as a signal that inflation will start rising and that interest rates should be raised.

Various factors are said to determine the level of the NAIRU. These can include factors such as the power of trade unions and of business but also the skills and 'employability' of the work force (the latter is lowered by a history of unemployment). The policy instruments overlap (e.g. reduce trade union power, but in the era of 'new monetarism', trade union power is no longer considered a problem), and initially seemed to involve a focus on education, skills, improving employability. This leads to declarations such as 'New Labour believes in a flexible labour market that serves employers and employees alike'.[13] This again involves what may be thought of as 'market imperfections'. For 'old monetarism', those imperfections were associated with the level of unemployment benefits, trade unions, minimum wage legislation etc. For 'new monetarism', the market failure is a lack of training and skills. It is well known that firms will tend to under-invest in training and skills. Training is costly for the firm and there is no guarantee that the person trained will stay with the firm for it to reap the benefits of that training. In the economics jargon, provision of training and skill formation are likely to suffer from market failure. However, whilst the 'new monetarism' at first seemed to be rather more humane

12. Estimate made by the Treasury's Chief Economic Adviser to House of Commons Treasury Committee, December 1996, as reported in J.Grieve Smith, 'Grasping the nettle: the problem of pay', *Renewal*, Vol 5, No 2, 1997, p38.
13. See, The Labour Party, *New Labour Deserves Better*, Labour Party 1997, p15.

than the 'old monetarism' (for example, emphasising skill formation rather than the reduction of benefits), this would be to overlook the implications of the 'welfare to work' programme with the reductions of benefits for lone parents and the threatened reductions in benefits for the disabled. This continues the tradition noted by Galbraith: to get the poor to work, reduce their income, to get the rich to work, raise their income. We should also be wary of appeals to flexible labour markets: this is a euphemism for short-term contracts, for temporary work and fluctuating wages. The aim should be for flexible organisations which can respond to change, but which provide stable employment and have reasons to provide training. The aim should also be for flexible workers who have a range of skills and undertake a range of jobs.

The approach of 'new monetarism' to economic policy has two fundamental weaknesses. First, the Bank of England, seeking to establish a reputation as an inflation hawk, will push up interest rates at (or before) the first signs of rising inflation. Unemployment below the NAIRU is taken as evidence that inflation will begin to rise, and the Bank of England steps in to deflate the economy. Since the election of 1997, the Bank of England's Monetary Policy Committee (MPC) has raised the rate of interest no less than five times, precisely on the grounds of the economy being overheated (this is at the time of writing, mid-December 1997). These implications of the operational independence of the Bank of England, a pre-requisite of the UK's membership of the European Monetary Union, will be replicated by the European Central Bank once the single currency is introduced in the EU. There is, thus, considerable deflationary bias introduced into the system. The prospect of inflation from a decline in unemployment leads to interest rates rising, slowing down the economy. But further, the slowing down and the high interest rates impact on investment, and that makes subsequent upswings more difficult to sustain as the expansion hits capacity constraints well before full employment is reached.

Second, while it is a worthy objective of economic policy to have people who are more 'employable', the question remains as to whether there will be sufficient capacity on which they can work and sufficient demand to buy the goods and services which they are capable of producing. Policies to ensure high levels of investment in plant and machinery as well as in people and to create productive capacity in the particularly deprived areas of many inner cities are required. It is also necessary to encourage a high level of demand, through government expenditure, exports and investment. If there is a budget deficit as a result of the higher government expenditure, so be it: it is a price well worth paying. In the longer run it may not even be a price. Higher economic activity would generate more government revenue and lower unemployment benefits, which should imply smaller deficit than otherwise. However, the conditions for membership of the single currency (the Maastricht criteria, including limits on budget deficits) would not allow such an expansion to take place. In any case, the likely over-valuation of sterling, emanating from the operation of the Bank of England, would adversely effect the generation of high levels of demand.

Blair has argued that, 'Unemployment is not just a social problem, but an economic problem as well. The Tories' indifference to the climb in long term unemployment in the 1980s and 1990s is indefensible. We must make a clear commitment to get long term unemployment down'.[14] This focus on the reduction of long term unemployment is indicative of 'new monetarism', as it sees long term unemployment as eroding skills and the work ethic, loosening ties with the labour market, but also not having any impact on inflation. Thus long-term unemployment can be reduced without risking inflation, but not short-term unemployment. Strategies to reduce long-term unemployment include the usual gamut of supply-side measures. But what is not included is any sense of where the jobs for the long-term unemployed are coming from, especially without reducing the jobs that would have been available for the short-term unemployed. The concentration of the long-term unemployed in particular areas requires that jobs be created in those areas: it is as much a problem of job creation as of employability.

'New monetarism' would be central to the operation of the European single currency. Monetary policy would be in the hands of an 'independent' European Central Bank ('independent' being a euphemism for undemocratic) which will have the objective of low (or zero) inflation, to be achieved through the manipulation of interest rates. Fiscal policy will remain in the hands of national governments, though constrained by the 3 per cent of GDP deficit rule (think what that would have meant in 1991 when in the face of recession the deficit in the UK rose to 8 per cent of GDP). Fiscal and monetary policies will be

---

14. Tony Blair, 1995, op.cit., p10.

uncoordinated: 'The third problem which undermined the effectiveness of monetary policy during the 1980s was the failure to use monetary and fiscal policy in a co-ordinated fashion'.[15] So what does the government do? It gives operational independence to the Bank of England, thus reducing the possibilities for the policy co-ordination! Whilst there are many other issues concerning the single currency (such as the lack of convergence between economies over a wide range of economic variables and institutional arrangements from levels of productivity and employment through to the arrangements for wage and price determination and the structures of the financial system, plus the lack of labour mobility between European economies in comparison with the United States), the centrality of the 'new monetarism' to the project should be seen as a major obstacle.

Financial markets have always posed problems for governments, especially Labour governments, and placed constraints, sometimes severe ones, on economic policy. The globalisation of financial markets and the very much greater flows across the exchanges have served to increase those constraints. But what is different about 'new monetarism' is the appearance of welcoming those constraints, or at least regarding them as benign. If the markets are all-knowing, then they serve the very useful purpose of keeping governments on the straight and narrow. This was expressed by Blair in the following: 'Errors in macroeconomic policy will be punished rapidly and without mercy' - financial markets are right, governments can be wrong.[16] Better to have the financial markets tell you that a policy is not credible than to implement the policy and find that it fails. We would all have to accept that financial markets are powerful and can make or break economies. A number of examples where financial markets imposed their will include Mexico in late 1994, South Korea, Thailand, and other Far Eastern economies in late 1997. These are cases where the economy concerned was pursuing neoliberal policies, especially financial liberalisation policies, but were nevertheless undermined by financial markets. Furthermore, sterling's membership of the ERM in the early 1990s is an example of financial markets welcoming sterling's entry into the mechanism, and then being largely responsible for its exit. Rather than seeking ways of reducing the

---

15. *Ibid*, p7.
16. Tony Blair, speech to the British American Chamber of Commerce, 11 April 1996.

power of financial markets, 'new monetarism' appears to welcome the guidance of financial markets.

Previous Labour governments have recognised the problem of low levels of investment. In the Labour Party manifesto there were passing references to the need to build up investment, though usually with reference to training and education. There is, however, little by way of clear proposals for increasing investment and creating the necessary capacity so that full employment can be restored. The little there is clearly suggests a policy of making the UK attractive to inward investment. 'With Labour, British and inward investors will find this country an attractive and profitable place to do business'.[17] If this has any meaning, it must be the first time that a Labour government has proclaimed that it seeks to shift income from wages to profits. Whatever the merits of inward investment, government policy should be directed towards ensuring that the gains of that investment accrue to the British people and not to the multinational enterprises. Further, there is little reason to think that inward investment will create jobs in areas of high unemployment, and does little to encourage local entrepreneurial activity: it is more like the promotion of a dependency culture.

The policies so far pursued by the new Labour government can be seen as the final triumph of monetarism and the defeat of Keynesian economic policies. The central concern of government policy is with inflation and with the appeasement of the financial markets, whose judgement on economic policies is accepted. The thrust of policy forgets two essential requirements for full employment: sufficient aggregate demand and adequate productive capacity. Only when those requirements are addressed will there be any prospect for the achievement of full employment.

We are grateful to Doreen Massey, Michael Rustin, Gary Slater and David Spencer for helpful comments.

---

17. Labour Party 1997, *op.cit.*, p15.

Future generations

A right way forward?

Mario Petrucci

Do the unborn have rights? Mario Petrucci considers this neglected issue and suggests ways in which it should be taken more seriously in social and political thought.

Unborn hands can't mark ballot papers, can't pay taxes. This inescapable fact of unlife goes a long way towards explaining why future generations are paid little more than lip service in political arenas. Except where capital can be made on acknowledging our natural concern for the young, future interests are generally demoted in favour of more urgent and accountable claims.

Outside the scripted narratives of science fiction, the future remains nebulous territory in the public psyche. Its peoples are an amorphous entity, called upon as the (assumedly) grateful beneficiaries of long-term projects, or press-ganged into uncontradicting service when rhetoric demands we be judged by some (usually traditional) standard. There is a vague sense of wishing to do them service, inherited - at least in part - from the Victorians' attempts to colonise and mould the future in their own image. But rarely does any exploration or rationalisation of these feelings occur beyond the delivery of abstract apostrophes.

The theoretical debate for rejecting or accepting future interests is similarly diffuse, languishing in an underexplored purlieu of the literature where disagreements over the nature and extent of our obligations to the future are politely - and occasionally - ruminated.[1] Contemporary philosophy has constructed no ethical edifice within which to house our moral obligation towards future generations. There is barely an outhouse. Because of this, I hope to provide here some possibilities that can act as starting points for further debate and political activism.

Life beyond the crib?

According to most major classical theories of ethics, it is nonsense to hold moral obligations towards people who do not exist. The basic arguments can be summed up in two ways. One arm is represented by Derek Parfit's 'Person-Affecting Principle', whereby you can't do wrong to someone if your actions don't affect them, a position held widely in much utilitarian thought.[2] Clearly, our actions cannot affect those with whom our lives do not overlap, who do not exist now, or who may never exist at all - or so the argument goes.[3] The other arm takes hold of the assertion that there can only be moral obligations between people if they're able to enter into negotiation and agreement, if there is some degree of mutual vulnerability keeping them subject to each other. In other words, a personal or social contract must be forcibly made. Extreme standpoints of this kind claim that the framework of morality itself will disintegrate if this prerequisite of moral reciprocity is not maintained. We are therefore free of moral obligation to the future because we cannot harm them, negotiate with them, or be taken to task by them.

But there is dissension in the ranks. Some radicalists have begun to argue that our obligations to future people are as binding as those we have towards the living, a position widely upheld (they claim) by 'moral intuitions'.[4] These

---

1. See the various arguments in R. Attfield, *The Ethics of Environmental Concern*, Blackwell, Oxford 1983; R. Sikora and B. Barry (eds), Obligations to Future Generations, Temple University Press, Philadelphia 1978. Also, Jere Paul Surber, 'Obligations to Future Generations: Explorations and Problemata', *Journal of Value Inquiry* 11, 1977, pp104-116.
2. Derek Parfit in R. Attfield, *op. cit.*
3. Attfield, *op. cit.*; D.W. Pearce and R.K. Turner, *Economics of Natural Resources and the Environment*, 1990, ch.15.
4. Attfield, *op. cit.*, pp95-97; B. Barry, 'Justice Between Generations', P.M.S. Hacker and J. Raz (eds), *Law, Morality and Society*, Clarendon Press, Oxford 1977, p268 et seq.

views run against the formulations of moral obligation given by Hume and Locke, and cut little water with more recent treatises by the likes of Nozick, Golding and Passmore. This disparity between moral intuition and classical theory is otherwise ignored by contemporary analysis, a negligence of staggering proportions when one considers the immense political, social and economic ramifications that would result if any consistent ethical position were to be taken up on this issue.

Rights?

One possible response towards the claims of future generations, assuming that such claims are valid, is to grant them rights. Rights represent a special emphasis on certain 'cardinal' interests in society, which they are designed to protect, whilst individuating our obligations towards them by assigning those rights to individuals. This protection is usually given moral priority over any negotiable goods. It would seem plausible to at least propose as candidates for rights any key interests that future generations may have. Since abstract entities such as corporations now possess rights, why not the unconceived? These putative rights can be interrogated in two ways:

i) Can future generations be said to possess rights at all, in any morally meaningful sense?
(ii) If future generations are legitimate bearers of rights, then which rights lay obligations upon this generation, and to what degree?

Most critics see the allocation of specific rights to future people as even more problematic than the concession of some vague moral ground. The arguments mostly follow on from those given earlier, and can be summarised as follows:

Temporality: Traditional ways of unpacking rights (in terms of interests, justifiable moral claims, or freedom) cannot apply to those who don't now exist, for reasons similar to those embodied by the Person-Affecting Principle. To speak of a future claim being considered now, or of a rights infringement in the absence of a bearer of that right, merely brings confusion. If we are honest, ascribing rights to future persons is really about meeting our own psychic concerns.[5]

Uncertainty: As far as future generations are concerned, what can we really know about them? We don't know who they will be, what they'll be like, what their needs will be, what will be good for them, what will be the nature and extent of their interests and expectations, or what moral frameworks they will judge their own actions by, let alone ours. We can't even be sure how many of them - if any - will exist, which makes it all but impossible to weigh their interests against our own.

Contingency: How can we be sure a so-called infringement of the rights of a future generation will actually materialise? Past actions of society then considered beneficial to the long-term 'common good' have had a range of consequences. For all we know, humanity may not even survive long enough to see the supposed infringements occur.

Individuality: Strictly speaking, rights are held and claimed by, or on behalf of, individuals. It may be that future generations can only meaningfully possess 'collective' rights, since the particular individuals involved are not known and cannot argue their case.

Lack of precedent: Conceding rights to future generations has no precedent in ethical theory.[6] If obligations to future generations do exist, it may be that other ethical frameworks are better suited to describing and meeting them.

This formidable array of objections might tempt us into the trap of believing that future generations cannot meaningfully be discussed in ethical terms. But strong counter-arguments exist.[7] We can bypass the problem of temporality, for example, by claiming that future generations possess rights now which can be claimed on their behalf by appointed representatives.[8] This isn't quite as fanciful

---

5. R.T. De George, 'The Environment, Rights and Future Generations', K.E. Goodpaster and K.M. Sayre (eds), *Ethics and Problems of the 21st Century*, 1979, pp93-104.
6. *Ibid.*
7. R. and V. Routley, 'Nuclear Energy and Obligations to the Future', *Inquiry* 21, 1978, pp133-179.
8. J. Feinberg, Conference at the University of Georgia (Feb 1971). Proceedings in W.T. Blackstone (ed), *Philosophy and Environmental Crisis*, 1974.

as it may at first seem. We can imagine plausible extensions and reinterpretations of contemporary cases where the rights of those who no longer exist are faithfully upheld.[9] Examples include wills and probates, and respect amongst friends and family for the expressed wishes of the dead. Such cases can be taken as confirmation that present existence is not a necessary condition for the ascription of present rights.[10]

Some factions of the 'Expanded Rights' lobby have already argued against temporality to make an initial case for including future generations in the sphere of moral concern.[11] Feinberg's touchstone paper on the extension of rights employs 'the interest principle' as its basis for rights assignation: the mentally inhibited, babies, animals and future generations may not be full moral agents, but they do have interests (a capacity to fare well or fare ill) and thus a right to their satisfaction.[12] Another fall-back position against the criticism of moral irreciprocity and the inability of future people to argue their case, is given by Regan.[13] He confers upon future generations the status of 'moral patients' whose rights can be claimed by proxy. The underlying point here is that a personal ability to press a claim or to understand a violation of interests is not a necessary condition for the possession of rights. We don't generally exclude from justice and care those who have no bargaining power or self-awareness.[14] This argument spills over into the problem of 'individuality'. After all, our own systems of rights and obligations aren't always person-specific, but often of a group nature, or identity-specific. We speak of the rights of children, or of minorities. In such cases, frameworks are established within which individuals - or their proxies - may make claim. Even if the rights of future generations were only to be of a collective nature, it should be possible to establish some framework similar to those currently in existence, with the appropriate resources to support it. There are difficulties, of course, with regard to the selection, pragmatics and impartiality of representation, but it isn't an insuperable task to arrive at an iterative long-term bill of rights for future generations based initially

9. A. Baier, 'The Rights of Past and Future Persons', in J. Desjardins and J. McCall (eds), *Contemporary Issues in Business Ethics*, 1985, pp171-183.
10. Attfield, *op. cit.*, p125. The 'Person Affecting Principle' may be found on p119.
11. Pearce and Turner, *op. cit.*
12. Blackstone, *op. cit.*
13. T.Regan, *The Case for Animal Rights*, Routledge, London 1988, p153.
14. Attfield, *op. cit.*

on broad principles designed to meet their likely and most basic needs.

Regarding the lack of precedent, perhaps our own generation is a special case. Our unprecedented predictive knowledge and environmental impact may give rise to new moral responsibilities against which future generations can, for the first time in history, legitimately make claim. We may also observe that the efforts of previous generations were not intended for our benefit alone: we therefore have a moral duty to pass on the inheritance intact. Such beliefs have institutional precedents in the form of bodies such as the National Trust.

An equal right to rights?

Even if all these counter-arguments are accepted, and the claim of future generations to certain basic rights is ratified, a profound problem remains. A system of inalienable rights simply cannot deal with cases where demands exceed resources, or where two sets of unbridgeable rights are in direct conflict.[15] This seems to be the major surviving weakness of a rights approach. It's essential, therefore, to explore what I term the 'problem of prioritisation' in rights allocation. I'll summarise now the various positions that can be taken up in cases where future needs compete with our own, or where they're too immense to be met by us without significant hardship.[16]

Temporality: People's basic needs (such as access to food and shelter) aren't likely to diminish with time, so shouldn't be downgraded simply by virtue of temporal location. Also, our own future rights and those of future generations reside in a similar moral category, since none of them yet exist. If we justify carrying our rights into our own personal futures, then rational consistency demands the same consideration be extended to future generations. Perhaps it's unfair to offer future generations equal footing in all such matters, since current demands can only be met by us, whilst liabilities to the future might reasonably be shared over a number of intervening generations.

---

15. Sikora and Barry, *op. cit.*; Surber, *op. cit.*
16. See G.S. Kavka, 'The Futurity Problem' in R.I. Sikora and B. Barry *op. cit.*, reprinted in E. Partridge (ed), *Responsibilities to Future Generations*, Prometheus Books, New York 1981, pp109-122; R.E. Goodin, 'No Moral Nukes', *Ethics* 90, 1980, pp417-449, (particularly p429).

Uncertainty/contingency: It's worthwhile remembering that we ourselves were once a 'future generation'. We might therefore prise some understanding from the ways in which the long (and short!) term policies of the past have ramified into our own present. In spite of (the less helpful forms of) post-modernism, historical analysis is not yet entirely defunct - that is to say, we can't claim total ignorance over the ways in which our current actions will affect future people and their rights. We needn't know the precise details of all possible universes to assert that the resources of two world wars might better have been deployed, that the release of untested virus strains from laboratories is best avoided, or that in fifty years' time most people will still need to eat. So, even if we could convince ourselves we had grounds for preferential rights over, say, fossil fuels, because future generations will probably be technologically superior and therefore possess alternatives, it isn't quite as easy to justify handing on a carcinogenic atmosphere or widespread contamination.

Having said this, it's wise to also take the best of post-modernism and admit that social analysis is problematic to say the least - even without its historical and dialectic dimensions - and always subject to a plurality of interpretations and a certain ineffability. Wanton or partisan extrapolations of 'historical' knowledge are therefore simply not on. Cultural interests are always in temporal flux: the wildernesses, for instance, that were once thought hostile and undesirable are now objects of conservation. All views of the future must remain hypothetical, to varying degrees.

It's important to point out at this stage that in deciding what to do - as opposed to what to avoid - we are also among the first generations for whom 'far-sighted' policies could back-fire on a global scale, as in the provision of long-term energy needs by a nuclear route.[17] Attfield makes it clear that our obligations to act on behalf of the future are lessened where known factors intervene to make our efforts likely to miscarry.[18] This is not to argue for inaction, but to note that the allocation of equivalent rights to resources between generations might only be justified where future benefits can reasonably be assured. However, the question of uncertainty cuts both ways and should also

17. De George, *op. cit.*
18. Attfield, *op. cit.*

extend to the 'they'll have found a solution by then' mentality which reigns conveniently and ominously supreme in popular thought. A more productive attitude towards future generations might consist of not inhibiting their flexibility of response to future circumstances.

Discounting the future

Another bias against the future can be found drowsing in the axiomatic nest of classical economics. The common practice of 'discounting' involves reducing the value of deferred capital as a function of time, due to considerations such as inflation and lost investment opportunities. This is nothing to do with wear and tear, but a way of saying that it is economically more efficient to have goods or capital now than at some time in the future. Similar arguments pertain to future costs. According to the discounting principle, all assets and costs depreciate by a given annual percentage - the 'discount rate' - whenever their future value is being considered (all other factors affecting their value remaining constant). The annual discount rate is usually equated to the official rate of return on economic investment, currently about 7 per cent.

Discounting is not altogether unjustified in certain cases, but the details of its application are a real bone of contention between ethical-radical and conservative economists. To begin with, discounting promotes near-termism by giving the here-and-now an inherent edge. Then there is the moral objection that all the long-term costs airbrushed to non-existence by the discount rate will nevertheless be very real indeed for the future generations who must suffer them. Indeed, where distant futures are concerned, discounting erodes the value of long-term investment and risk-prevention to practically nil, oblivious of any irreversibilities which may result from our failure to act now. A case in point is the corporate rationale behind the dumping of nuclear waste. If the waste can be made secure for a sufficient length of time, then the cost of any clean-up - however vast - can effectively be glossed to zero. For example, if we take an annual discount rate of 10 per cent and assume the waste containment can be absolutely guaranteed for 250 years (which it can't), then the estimated equivalent cost to society of one trillion pounds clean-up (at today's value) in the year 2247 is just £3.64. Evidence - if ever it was needed - that economic rationality can be sublimely savage. The practice of discounting in project assessment remains a serious barrier to the just allocation of inter-generational responsibilities and benefits.

Another tack taken by those arguing diminished responsibility towards the future is that the standard of living continues to rise; this is surely the best inheritance we can hope to leave. In reply, I suggest a closer look at those breaches of basic human rights and social equity which are occurring right now as a direct consequence of the growth modes we favour, along with a consideration of the degree to which similar rights will be infringed in the future as a result of the global unsustainability and long-term risks which current practices precipitate. Incremental benefits for the few may be somewhat irrelevant to the bulk of a future generation whose life support systems are in collapse.

Future rights - to the head of the queue?

What about the arguments for preferential treatment of future generations?[19] Those who currently enjoy a privileged lifestyle (that is, most of the Northern hemisphere) could begin by reconsidering the moral imperative 'from those who have much, much is expected', a redistributive call which could be applied between, as well as within, generations. In addition, if, as it seems, imminent future generations will out-number us, perhaps they should be given a louder voice than ours in resource claims. Instead of diminishing our obligations to future generations, uncertainty over the future can actually enhance their rights on the basis that their (unknown) options could be more limited than our own. Finally, if entities such as animals and future generations are indeed 'moral patients', it may be argued that their rights should carry priority over ours because of their relative vulnerability.

Right on?

It's clear from the foregoing discussion that a wide range of standpoints is possible with respect to future rights, depending on which arguments and counter-arguments are accepted. At one extreme no rights should be granted at all, and even weaker moral obligations may not apply; at the other extreme, equal consideration is required in all cases of equivalent need, with many instances where the rights of future generations, including non-humans, should be put

---

19. Baier, *op. cit.*; T.S. Derr, 'The Obligation to the Future', in E. Partridge, *op. cit.*

first regardless of cost. Both of these pole-points are, I feel, difficult to defend. I present instead three compromise positions, stated formally and in order of increasing emphasis on future rights. Between them, I hope to cover the range of palatable positions.

Position A (conservative)

Let us attempt to extend rights into the future, but prioritise them according to the likelihood that the rights-holders and their claims will exist. Obligations to meet these rights should be borne by those individuals and groups most responsible for bringing the claims/claimants into existence. It follows that our primary responsibilities lie towards our own (human) generation and its immediate descendants. The pragmatic problems of future rights, and the surrounding difficulties of uncertainty and valid representation, mean that such rights can only be formulated in terms of broad principles and intentions.

Position B (far-minded)

Although the interests of future generations are contingent and uncertain, it is not unreasonable to assume that some future generations will exist, and that their basic size, needs, behaviours, capacities and interests are likely to be extensions of our own (at least for proximate generations). It is also clear from studied experience that past strategies are capable (at least to some extent) of facilitating or hindering future social activity. Furthermore, we now have sufficient capability to alter the course of global processes and a sufficient means to understand and monitor them, that continued inaction on the grounds of ignorance or impotence cannot reasonably be justified. Doing harm to future generations no longer requires wilful appropriation, but mere carelessness or indifference, for which we ought to be held culpable.

There are therefore firm ethical grounds for considerable future-oriented action (or avoidance of inaction) on our part, especially where the long-term consequences could be serious.[20] We accept that the rights and interests of future generations carry partial, sometimes equal, and occasionally greater weight relative to our own. At the very least, we should bequeath the means by which future generations can meet their most certain and urgent needs, and through

---

20. R. and V. Routley, *op. cit.*

which they can retain a flexibility of response.

Having said this, we cannot be held responsible for what we genuinely do not and cannot know. The represented claims of future generations are to be upheld only where our liability, or the benefits of remedial action, are reasonably certain. Neither should far-mindedness blind us to our necessary obligations to the living. It might, then, be efficient to give priority to those rights which service the primary human needs both of present and future generations (e.g. equitable land ownership). However, caution should be exercised in allocating future rights in areas where attitudes can substantially change (wilderness conservation provides a case in point). Claims of distant generations can be partially discounted, but not where basic needs are concerned. Wherever possible, we should avoid activities that threaten future livelihoods, especially where such activities merely serve our secondary needs. Where justified, the burden for the future should be shared with intermediate generations, but environmental irreversibility remains the full responsibility of whoever brings it about, whether directly or indirectly. It is to be debated whether, and to what degree, rights ought to be allocated to future non-human species.

Position C (future-oriented)

It is morally repugnant to burden future generations with life-threatening dangers so that we can enjoy extra increments of comfort, and reprehensible to knowingly bequeath risks and harms to future life-support systems. A precautionary principle should be adopted, along with ongoing investments of all kinds to protect the interests of the near and distant future. Discounting should only be used - if at all - in a limited and strictly ethical set of cases. It will be necessary to distinguish between needs and wants (as in the 'need' for central heating, personal motor cars or tobacco). Abstentions which improve the prospects for future life on the planet are to be embraced as a sign of civilised consciousness. Uncertainty over the future means that we can sometimes allocate lower priority to some of the rights of future generations, but we are not thereby justified in wasteful or unnecessary consumption of resources they may need. Our greed, indifference or irresponsibility should not be allowed to cause unnecessary future suffering or deprive future generations of things they could reasonably expect to have. They have a right to safely enjoy the basic means of a quality existence, as far as we can ensure it. However, there is no moral obligation for self-sacrifice on our part where its results are unclear or where the resources - directly or indirectly - could be redistributed to meet the imperative needs of current generations. The rights of future non-human species should also be taken into account, particularly where the required resources are not essential to us.

Clearly, much debate is needed to determine which of these positions stands up best to scrutiny, particularly in cases where the interests of present and future generations clash. I'm aware that my approach has been fairly general and that I haven't said much about the precise pragmatics of putting these positions into effect. Quite apart from needing a book to even begin to go into that, so little exists on the subject that some broad and tentative ethical guidelines represent, in themselves, a major step forward.

Perhaps more serious are the various straw terms strewn in my wake: 'primary', 'secondary' 'needs'. It's the meaning of such terms that I hope will be a central part of the debate. I'm certain, too, that some of you will have glimpsed, lumbering behind this article, a Frankensteinian monster of endless and burdensome litigation, into which - it may seem - I am attempting to breathe an unnatural a-temporal life. Questions also remain as to how many generations ought to be considered, how their relative weightings can be estimated, and how best to select proxies to represent future claims. Most importantly, how are the claims to be enforced or their proceeds delivered?

I willingly raise these spectres because I believe that ultimately the basic rights of future generations can probably be developed in relatively simple ways and incorporated into policy and debate as another factor alongside the many which already exist, or as substitutes for some of the more facile considerations upon which bureaucracy currently insists. Some of the required ideas are not entirely new. We've already woven hereditary law into the fabric of society and taken the trouble to establish bodies such as the NERC and the Human Rights Commission. Can't these be improved, extended, adapted? An example of a first step for Position B, say, might be the creation of some kind of 'futures' fund held in trust for prospective claimants, where the multinationals and governments of each generation are taken to court by proxies and instructed to pay fines on the basis of negotiated and ethical criteria of infringed interest. The problems of enforcement would be no worse than for existing international law, severe though they are. The rampant legal bureaucracy to which rights-oriented approaches can sometimes lead, particularly when improperly framed and pursued, may be avoidable and is, in any case, the subject of a much broader social critique.

However, these difficulties might suggest to some that a rights approach to future generations may not be the best vehicle after all for dealing with our moral intuitions towards them. Nevertheless, it is now important to ascertain, quickly, the pressing environmental instances and risks to which future-oriented action could be applied. Pollution, stratospheric ozone depletion, the build-up of toxic wastes, the exhaustion of vital resources, the ongoing capacity for nuclear war, destruction of key habitats, species extinction, global warming ... these are among the dozens of ways in which current human activity could ramify detrimentally, and on an unprecedented scale, into the prospects of future species, including our own. Regardless of whether or not a rights-based approach turns out to be best, we must begin to assess various ethical frameworks for their suitability in protecting the interests of long-term humanity.

In some cases then, rights might provide part of a solution, at least in principle, to the problem of devising an ethical framework for the protection of future interests. There may indeed be good sense in granting future generations the right of equal access to 'basics' such as food, usable air and water, fertile land, space, shelter, and the essential ecosystems which provide global stability. But we must also begin to see all of our cultural, economic and political behaviours as part of the 'raw material' (or pollutants) which future generations will have to process. It may be equally important to bequeath future generations a set of constructive and compassionate social attitudes, or an international political economy rooted in justice, or - dare I say it? - wisdom, as it is to provide them with tangible resources or technical and scientific expertise.

Whence the will?

Future-oriented activity will require the backing of new ethical theory, for example in collective approaches to rights and obligations, areas which remain conceptually and legally obscure.[21] But theory is not enough. There must also

---

21. De George, *op. cit.*

be strong public and political will. Urgency and motivation for change must come from somewhere other than personal discomfort or imminent personal destruction, which may never be imminent enough. Perhaps we can extend and transcend that most fundamental concern regarding future generations: that for one's children and grandchildren.

Perhaps not; I fully accept that the translation of individual motivations into collective action is tough at the best of times. Beneficence towards future generations (via a regard for environmental preservation, for instance) has spilled across national barriers for decades and yet no world institutions exist equal to the task of addressing intergenerational rights. However, this is no reason for allowing our critical acuity to lapse. The new definitions of 'social welfare' and economic 'optimality', cast increasingly in terms of near-term economic strictures and cost-benefit analyses, rubbish the interests of future generations, particularly through discounting. The academic centres and political radicalists should at least exercise a voluble vigilance.

But even if a wider debate were to be kick-started, it is probable that nothing short of a revolution in activist compassion will lead to future generations being taken seriously in political and economic arenas. I understand, too, that there are those for whom an article on the rights of future generations may seem little more than futile wordplay when set against a backdrop of intimidating, and growing, social disequity both within and between nations as they are now. The issue may appear secondary in a world where economic, moral and ecological crises are deepening and expanding on a global scale. Meanwhile, economic efficiency and the free market stand supreme as arbiters of the public interest and its rights, and near-termist individualism continues to swell as the cultural hegemonic. There may also be a post-neo-liberal backlash to contend with, developing against a perceived glut of litigation and rights-sans-obligation, and for whose protagonists the projection of rights into time may be one straw too many.

And yet, to preserve its good health, ethics needs to chew on more than what is currently popular, achievable or enforceable - war and poverty may persist, but most of us continue to argue against them in principle. In addition, a compassion and respect for the future does nothing to negate that first and crucial task of working for social justice now. It may even help to resensitise us to the present. In any case, it's worth remembering that when politicians do talk about delivering on rights and social justice, it may well be distant generations they have in mind.

Thinking with music

Angela McRobbie

To relate music to cultural theory is not enough. Angela McRobbie argues that adopting a more materialist analysis will allow us to sample the artistry and literary voice of current music makers.

Who is that by?

Nowhere is the marriage between art and science more happily secured than in the extraordinary profusion of cheap-to-produce popular musics which over the last fifteen or so years have created a music-society to rival and even outstrip the image-society in which we now live. This forces a reassessment of what music means in everyday life, but so prolific is the output of so many different genres, which converse with and against each other, that few critics seem capable of creating a credible map, or writing a story of contemporary pop. Music-making defiantly slips the net of language, setting itself, as Susan Sontag memorably put it, back in the 1960s, 'against interpretation'. Current music styles leapfrog backwards and forwards in time, snatching phrases, chords and strains of sound from unlikely sources, placing one on top of the other, and making issues of authorship and ownership irrelevant. 'Who is that by?' becomes an absurdly naive question. These musics play teasing, competitive games with the audience, for whom, listening on the car radio or even half submerged in the local swimming pool, there is always the chance that they will never hear the same track again. (For a moment, last summer, I thought of getting out of the water at the Archway pool in North London, to ask the DJ/swimming attendant the name of the hip-hop track that was playing. Its fluid inter-play of spoken word and backing track so evoked the bare-bone aesthetics of rap that it was good enough to drown in.)

Hip hop and dance musics propose newness, not just out of the application of bedroom size computer technology to old, discarded fragments of sounds, but also by forging a different relationship with their audiences. So energetically bound up are they with their own musical inventiveness, with what can, at the present moment, be done with music, that the DJs, the musicians and the producers, can virtually ignore the audience, in the same arrogant way that early punk did. So dispersed and fragmented, so volatile and widely spread, are the various audiences for contemporary music, that it seems almost pointless to think, who will this please? who will want to buy this record? This allows music to turn in on itself, and enjoy a moment of almost sublime self-confidence. This challenge to the audience is reflected in the challenge to the critic - or to the sociologist - we too seem suddenly redundant. What role is there now for criticism or analysis?

Indeed our critical vocabulary seems sadly lacking. None of the old words, like collage, montage, or postmodernism, seem capable of capturing the velocity and scale of this output. Likewise, the older ways of making sense of music by placing different styles into different categories, or by posing the commercial against the creative or experimental, or by talking about white or black music as though they were quite distinct, are equally inappropriate. Now, in the late 1990s, we have to start with an assumption of musical hybridity, with global cultural cross-over and profound inter-penetrations of style, coupled with a reliance on often quite basic machines to engineer a quality of D-I-Y eclecticism which even the huge and wealthy record companies have trouble knowing what to do with. Music, in short, has become 'artificially intelligent'.

Faced with the sheer challenge which music production poses, music writing and commentary in the more academic journals has actually pursued a fairly predictable course. The claim that current dance music styles appear to embrace a refusal of meaning, in the same way that they suggest a refusal of authorship and authenticity, is patently banal and unsatisfactory; and the conclusion which follows, which sees only political nihilism in sharp contrast to the political verve of punk, is equally fallacious and ahistorical.

Jeremy Gilbert has recently argued that 'However nihilistic they may have seemed at the time, not even Joy Division ... can really be located outside this discourse of protest'.[1] But the problem with this kind of account is that it posits a style of music, i.e. punk, even in its most nihilistic form, as being inherently close to politics, as though politics was this quantifiable, identifiable thing at the centre of social life. Current dance music in comparison pursues a logic of pure pleasure rather than politics, and thus confirms the essentially apolitical identity of young people in Britain in the late 1990s. Gilbert explains this in terms of the rave generation's frustration with 'mainstream political culture'.

> 'Music, in short, has become "artificially intelligent"'

Rave too is nihilistic, but it just, and no more, manages to rescue itself from the slur of having no politics whatsoever by refusing at least to share the nostalgic stage of national pride with Blur, Oasis and the other white boys of Britpop. In a similar vein the search for politics continues in Hemment's suggestion that 'The ecstatic dance is not in itself political, but it is a micropolitical event - an intervention in the formation of desire'.[2] Finally, Hesmondhalgh warns against a too easy confirmation of the democratic potential of dance music on the grounds of these same features of authorless music, imagined and produced largely outside the corporate cultures of the big music companies.[3] This is misleading, he argues, because it overlooks how dance music producers also get sucked into the star mythology of name DJs and the attraction of a record deal with a major company. Yet, despite this, Hesmondhalgh still wants to hold the torch for dance. Even though drum and bass has become 'yuppie cocktail music', he acknowledges in this music the 'often thrilling mixture of the dark and the uplifting'. In all three cases, and indeed across the field of writing academically about music, where it is recognised that, in some complicated way, something political is at stake, there is this same tension.

It is certainly not satisfactory to discount the political dynamic from the viewpoint that 'it's just music, after all'; nor are most left critics willing to adhere to the argument that the writing and the discussion somehow spoil the whole

---

1. J. Gilbert, 'Soundtrack for an Uncivil Society; Rave Culture, The Criminal Justice Act and the Politics of Modernity', *New Formations*, No 31, 1997.
2. D. Hemment, 'e is For Ekstasis', *New Formations*, No 31, 1997.
3. D. Hesmondhalgh, 'The Cultural Politics of Dance Music', *Soundings*, Issue 5, Spring 1997.

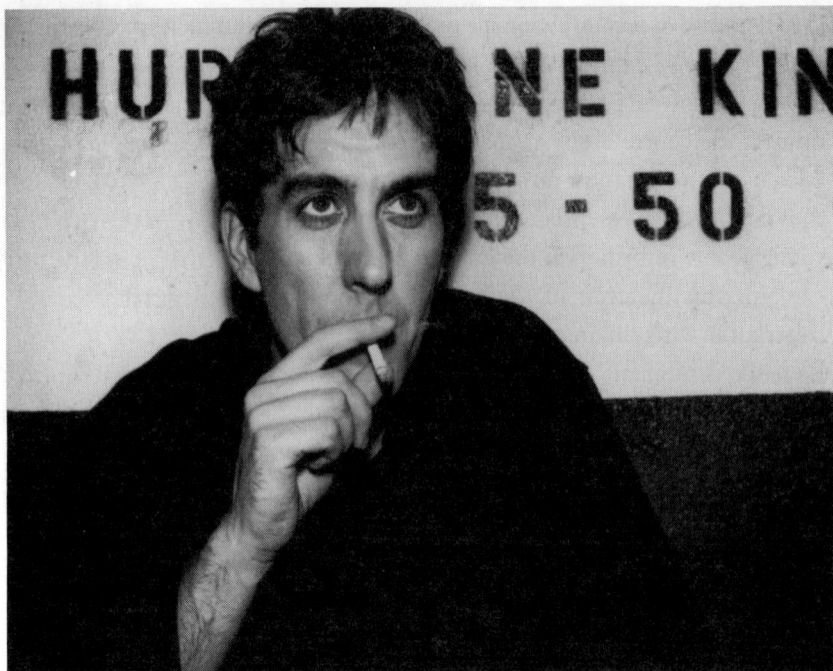

Terry Hall by Elaine Constantine

experience, that it robs the music of its whole reason to exist (as one of my own students recently put it). Perhaps the approach should be not to search around for a political and theoretical vehicle of such sophistication that it does justice to the significance of the phenonemon (which is how the presence of Deleuze and Guattari in the footnotes inevitably appears) but rather to be more realistic about the politics of music and the people who make the music, and adopt a more pragmatic, sociological approach, based on the question, what can academics say or do which might be useful? This would not mean the courting of political approval from a government attuned to the significance of the culture industries (indeed with a Culture Industries Strategy high on the agenda), by producing a string of policies, or 'good ideas' out of a hat. Quite the opposite, it might well mean the asking of very awkward questions of a government determined to use pop to look modern. But neither would such an approach simply succumb to the temptation to replace politics with theory, as though 'making sense' is achieved exclusively at that point where some convincing analogies can be drawn between a musical form and the frequently opaque writing of a number of French philosophers (enjoyable though such an attempt might be) .

Livelihoods in music

The more politically relevant point is surely that music today is also a place of employment, livelihoods and labour markets. This fact is obscured because being creative remains in our collective imaginations a sort of dream-world or utopia, far apart from the real world of earning a living; and the irony is that the philosophers are as spellbound by the idea of art and creativity as the rest of us. Baudrillard, for example, is reported as having said that the real attraction of retirement is that it means he can become a real writer, an artist no less. The popular music industry has drawn on the conventional language of genius, talent and charismatic personality, which is how modern society has understood the role of the artist. The artist is the romantic outsider whose exceptional gifts are manifest in how different he (occasionally she) is from the rest of us. But this is now a hopelessly anachronistic way of understanding music (and art) production in Britain in the 1990s. For a start there are a lot more people making music and hoping to earn a living from doing so. This is no longer a completely futile dream. The old jobs, which for many people meant a lifetime of unrewarding labour, have gone for ever, and there has been instilled into a younger generation, at some deep level, a determination for work to mean something more than a hard slog, for work to become a labour of love, a source of creative reward, a sort of poetics of living. For working-class boys (less so girls) without qualifications, it's become one possible thing to do, to turn youth culture into a job creation scheme. Too easily, in the demonic media-typecasting of young, often black, males on the fringes of criminality, do we forget the small humiliations and indignities of low paid, low status labour.

What an escape then, to move into music. It has been through this process of 'choosing culture' that the discovery of talent, imagination and even musical genius has occurred, in some cases transporting the individual from a career in crime (e.g. the rap artist Coolio) in the space of one record. In Britain the startlingly diverse and imaginative urban soundscapes of Manchester and Glasgow, Bristol and London, are an index of the scale of wastage which was (and still is) the mark of a class divided society, where middle-class children had (and have) every ounce of talent nurtured like a precious thing as a matter of course while the rest could quite easily have never known they had it in them. But even this does not exhaust the issues posed by the changes brought about by the culture society. How much music and how many musicians can the new culture-society accommodate? What kind of livings are being made? How can we gauge the span of talent and creativity? Who judges what constitutes musical genius? Indeed this line of enquiry can even be taken to the opposite extreme by suggesting that, at some level, to those now doing the producing, the questions, how good is it? ... Or, is it great art? are somehow less relevant. These are replaced instead by a sense of exploring further some very particular musical direction in a way which is uninterrupted by other, commercial constraints. We can see this particularly in the new musics being produced by figures like Roni Size and his colleagues and also Bjork.

With creative work now accounting for a much greater number of livelihoods, it may well be that in the process some of the old romantic notions have already slipped by the wayside. Artistic work has become more ordinary, it has been edged off its pedestal and turned into more common currency. It's not just that the art schools are churning out more graduates; further down the hierarchy there are any number of BTEC courses in sound production, studio engineering and computer programming, and the students who sign on for these have been mixing tracks in their bedrooms since they were twelve, and see quite clearly that electronics and engineering no longer mean working for the Electricity Board or for British Steel. The emphasis on the skill rather than on stardom does not mean that the utopian dynamics of these new apprenticeships for the night-time economies of dance and club culture are denied. Quite the reverse. Here we have, with the growth of *cultural capitalism*, something similar to the scenario Marx himself looked forward to: cooking, looking after the children and doing the ironing in the morning, writing lyrics and composing tracks on the home computer in the afternoon, and playing them for money in the evening! Caspar Melville describes how this happens in the world of drum and bass. 'It is not unusual for producers like Grooverider and 4Hero to make a piece of music in the daytime and play it 'out' at a club in the evening'.[4]

---

4. C. Melville, 'New Forms and Metal Headz; Jungle, Black Music and Breakbeat Culture', Unpub MA Dissertation Goldsmiths College, London 1997.

Morrisey by Rankin

How this kind of activity will work out in the post-welfare society remains to be seen. How much of the labour market can culture mop up? What kind of livings are there to be made in this cultural society? Are we witnessing the emergence in Britain of a new kind of low pay, labour intensive, cultural economy comprising of a vast network of freelance and self-employed 'creative people'? What sort of issues for government will be thrown up by the emergence of this kind of workforce as a long term phenomenon? Are they all dutifully paying their national insurance stamps? Have they already attended to their private pension plans? How does self-employment tally with the high cost of parenting? It's doubly difficult to get a real grip on these economics when they encompass such vast differences of income, from the now incredible wealth of The Prodigy to the modest living of Grandmaster Flash, for example. At the same time, what all of these performers (including the 12 year olds in their bedrooms) have in common is the possibility of producing cheap music through having access to sophisticated, home-based computer equipment.

The opportunities made available by these machines were spotted early on by figures like Grandmaster Flash, who learnt how to refine the art of mixing from the electronics course he was doing at technical school, and then proceeded to combine this knowledge with his curiosity for old records, which stemmed from his fascination with his father's record collection, locked away and out of reach of children's hands. As he said to David Toop, 'I would tiptoe up to the closet, turn the knob, go inside the closet and take a record.'[5] Being able to make music within the budget of pocket money and a Saturday job has also been a key factor in the prodigious expansion of tracks, twenty years after the birth of hip hop. It is how the first Prodigy album was cut, with Liam Howlett literally walking in off the street to the record company with a sequence of rave songs recorded in his bedroom. This is now common history, but the celebrity culture which almost immediately gears itself up for marketing musical success obscures what the local economies look like in the longer term. As far as I know, no attempt has been made to chart, for example, how current DJ careers are pursued in Britain, even how many of them there are plying their trade, and how sustainable these careers are.

An avant-garde of the self taught?

But obviously all this activity does count, more than just economically. Contemporary music culture embraces the banal and the sublime, but because most popular music still registers in the cultural hierarchies as 'untutored' or 'untrained', associated with talent, emotion and sensuality, its cerebral and socio-economic significance is often overlooked. (In a recent *Desert Island Discs* Sue Lawley (rather snootily) asked Jools Holland if he was 'self-taught'.) Critics can make all sorts of claims on behalf of the emotional power of popular music but rarely, if ever, do they dare propose a thinking role. As French sociologist Pierre Bourdieu would explain, if it's sensual and immediately gratifying, then it must

---

5. D. Toop, *The Rap Attack*, Serpents Tail 1984.

belong to the lower social classes, and thus be perceived as incapable of the depth and complexity found in the high arts and enjoyed by the educated social classes. It's been up to black writers in Britain like Paul Gilroy to demonstrate just how much thinking there is in black music. Such music can hardly contain the investment of artistry and politics and history and literary voice, so that, as an aesthetic, it is, by definition, spilling out and over-flowing, excessive, a first destination for social commentary, dialogue and rap which leaves those of us still caught in the 'prison house of language' far behind. But no establishment person on the quality press or elsewhere ever gives it the accolade of calling it a spectacular avant-garde, which is what it is. (Though it is also perhaps true that the popular, black idiom of this kind of musical activity also exposes the underpinnings, limits and exclusions of the term 'avant-garde'.)

> 'No establishment person ever gives black music the accolade of calling it a spectacular avant-garde'

It's not just music which is directly connected with black culture which provides a language of analysis and critique for its practitioners. Popular music in Britain provides an accessible, relatively open aesthetics for those who want to play. It can be something to think with and with which to explore class and history, city and space, sexuality, identity and tradition. And it is because this capacity has been grabbed as a kind of philosophical lifeline by some of the most interesting figures in this particular urban, post-war landscape, that much music means more than just pop. The way in which British pop has become particularly aware of its capacity for reflecting on all sorts of sexual anxieties, as well as other national obsessions, has been commented on since the early 1980s. The Pet Shop Boys and Morrissey are usually held up as prime exemplars of this, masters of surface poise, gentle irony, and explorers of white, polite, masculinity. There is a problem however when debate gets narrowly focused on the work of performers like these 'big names'. It becomes even more difficult to shift from a mode which considers their work and its meanings, and how these develop, where they come from, to one which is concerned with livelihoods and politics. So enormous is their personal wealth, they hardly have to worry about paying their mortgages or about what will happen if they get sick. The challenge then is to find ways of making connections between these, and other, success stories and the question of employment in music, and by extension in the culture industries. We can begin to do this, I would argue, by returning to questions of social class (as well as gender and ethnicity), history and biography.

Histories of music, politics of class

Three useful examples of how music can function as a way of thinking as well as a place of working came to my attention almost by chance last summer. I felt like reading about music again, and I was suddenly overtaken by a desire to go to hear music in the way I used to, when in the early 1980s in Birmingham there was such a rich musical crossover of reggae (Steel Pulse), disco (Sheila B Devotion), punk, and two-tone, as well as various well intended efforts at neo-Marxist pop. I re-read Simon Reynolds' influential *Blissed Out,* and found myself absorbed in his interview with Morrissey.[6] It showed Morrissey to be remarkably aware as a child that pop culture provided him with a kind of personalised map, a way of making sense of place, identity and existence. He told Reynolds how at the age of six he had his own magazine ... 'listening to the Top 30 every Tuesday only to run off instantly to the typewriter in order to compile my own personal Top 30 which totally conflicted with how the world really was ... It was a Top 30 of contemporary records, but the new entries were very unlikely, and obviously I favoured certain musicians, like T Rex'. This does not simply repeat to us what we already know about how popular culture has replaced nursery rhymes and fairy tales as a source of image, narrative and information, it also reveals an incredibly intelligent child looking to the charts as a way of working things out. In a more middle-class environment this no doubt would be gently discouraged. But in a single parent and class dislocated household, Morrissey was free to consume as much pop as he wanted. You get the impression of him being a rather pompous, old-fashioned child, giving pop his full unbridled attention.

A week later *The Guardian* ran a lengthy interview with Terry Hall, who had started off with The Specials and then set up the Fun Boy Three, and has recently released an excellent new album, *Laugh.*[7] This was a distressing story of a working-class boy making it into the local grammar school, only to be perceived as socially vulnerable by a teacher, who then subjected

---

6. S. Reynolds, *Blissed Out*, Serpents Tail 1990.
7. *The Guardian Weekend Supplement*, 10 July 1997 .

Jah Wobble by John Sleeman

him, along with another 13 year old, to kidnapping and sexual abuse. Unable to describe to his parents back home on the council estate what had happened to him, his school work went out the window and his days at grammar school were numbered. His talent was only able to surface inside the 'safer' confines of Coventry's grim and hard edged two-tone youth cultures of the early 1980s; here he wrote *Ghost Town*, a classic single which conjured up the history of black ska music by allowing it to gently haunt the outskirts of the song, envisaging and documenting the new intersections of black and white youth in Britain's inner cities.

The same week that this interview was published I slipped into a sweatbox in Islington to hear Jah Wobble's *Invaders of the Heart* play on one of the hottest nights of the year. It was a great performance in the King's Head, with a line up of reggae musicians and the drummer Jaki Liebezeit from Can. Wobble's bass playing (and his looming, expressionless, physical presence) led and connected the whole set, from a pared down jazz introduction, through a reggae section which combined Celtic instruments and Blakeian lyrics, through to a solid dance dub ending. The thudding bass line also told a story of class and history, of manual labour and then later of urban multi-culturalism. In his earlier incarnation with John Lydon this was put to spectacular effect in the first Public Image single (I forgot I had it, but recently rediscovered it in my box of records). The dark rumble (miles more ominous than anything The Prodigy have come up with), combined with Lydon's psychotic screechings, make it one of the most memorable (and influential) records ever made.

Wobble had done a number of extended interviews following the release of his most recent work.[8] He recalled walking out of a shabby, run-down East London school ('this was no Dead Poet's Society') and stumbling into Lydon with whom he then went on to share a squat. Eventually he picked up a bass guitar left lying around by Sid Vicious. Interwoven with this narrative was another one, of Dickensian cityscapes, of fifteen mile hikes round Lea Valley, to Greenwich and back to Cambridge Heath Road, of reading Yeats in Shadwell public library, of parents and grandparents who made their living from the river and its trade, of falling into music after falling out of hopeless jobs. He also told of abandoning music for a spell after Public Image and taking a job with the London Underground, and then finding his way back into music, and rediscovering his ability and talent and a sense that it couldn't be wasted.

Apart from the fact that this particular story vividly illustrated the cultural studies work of at least three of my colleagues, produced over the last twenty years - including Phil Cohen's seminal essay on youth cultures and the break up of the working-class community in East London, Hebdige's still magnificent structuralist reading of punk and also Willis's *Learning to Labour*[9] - all three interviews prompted more general questions about how academics engage with the sort of people who have been living and breathing what we scholars then write about or analyse. For example, it seems scandalous, after

---

7. *The Guardian Weekend Supplement*, 10 July 1997.
8. E. Fox, 'Songs of Innocence and Experience', *The Guardian Weekend Supplement*, 7 September 1998; and S. Feay, 'Here Comes The Stubble', *The Independent on Sunday*, 1 June 1997.

thirty years of comprehensive education, and the so-called decline of class society and its replacement by the consumer culture, that there remains a need to draw attention to the forces which continue to conspire against young people having access to forms of encouragement, and to finding ways of making good use of their talent. To be still in the business of showing the obstacles overcome, and the sheer contingency of achieving against a backdrop of active discouragement, is as politically demoralising as it is potentially patronising.

'It is very hard to survive in the long term in the freelance economy'

Better however to run that risk than to disappear entirely into the more intellectually tantalising but politically less useful project of searching for a theoretical language to measure up to the dizzying brilliance of contemporary music making. Of course the one should not counteract the other. But the stakes are high when (mostly male) academics set themselves the task of making sense of modern music. They are, it seems, haunted by the image, style and reputation of the (usually white) music journalist (again, you only have to check the references for the mentions of the halcyon days of the NME). In this context the writing has to somehow be a parallel text to the music. This is a boy's language which avoids at all costs soft subjects like those raised above, in favour of a breakneck breakdown of mutating styles, names, gadgets and equipment. Alternately, the aim is to elevate the music to the realm of the philosophical by introducing poetic fragments from Foucault, Deleuze or Guattari. This would be more welcome if the authors were willing to take their arguments further and ask what exactly it means, that the ecstatic, dancing, raving bodies of working-class boys (girls have always danced) in some field off the M74 correspond at some level to the 'bodies without organs' which are so central to Deleuze's concept of the social? Or indeed to challenge the new hegemony of the 'superhuman' black body and the power attributed to it in contemporary hip hop music, as Gilroy has recently and provocatively suggested.[10] But even the inclusion of these questions should not overshadow

---

9. P. Cohen, *Rethinking The Youth Question*, Macmillan, 1996; D. Hebdige, *Subculture; The Meaning of Style*, Methuen 1979; P. Willis, *Learning To Labour*, Saxon House 1979.
10. P. Gilroy, 'After The Love Has Gone'; Bio-politics and Etho-poetics in the Black Public Sphere', A. McRobbie (ed), *Back To Reality? Social Experience and Cultural Studies*, Manchester University Press 1997.

other issues, such as those involved in earning a living, or learning a skill in the new culture industries. The Creative Task Force, for instance, might well find itself confronted with more challenges than it has so far anticipated in all the rounds of hand-shaking. Alan McGhee, a member of the Task Force and manager of Oasis, has suggested that young musicians might be spared the pressure to find a proper job while receiving the Jobseeker's Allowance. Others are talking about the revival of the Enterprise Allowance Scheme, while my own recent research on creative workers in the fashion industry has shown clearly how hard it is to survive in the longer term in the freelance economy, never mind put money into a pension fund. So the current flowering of talent and energy across the creative industries will need more than just symbolic support, it will require a post-industrial strategy which, in its most hopeful mode, might mean that among those less supported by their own 'cultural capital', less is left to chance.

Thanks to Jah Wobble for his useful comments.

Five poems

Abroad

Even by the outskirts of Calais it's like being let loose
in a sweet shop - all those old favourites I'd forgotten
the taste of: *Rappel! Prix des carburants.* I roll them round
on my tongue, gob-stoppers of sounds I can't get enough of.
Virages sur dix kilometres. Aire du champs du drap d'or.
They melt on my breath into much more than recognition.
This is reclamation, primitive as pronouns, possessives.
But I keep it to myself, mouth them out of the window
under the Butterworth adagio you're tuned to, remembering
your mother's endless reciting of every road sign:
Give way. Reduce speed now. She'd haul in each letter
like a life-line. With amazement which was not quite delight
(her hold wasn't sure enough) she'd arrive at comprehension.
It drove us all mad. But she wasn't. She was abroad,
trying to recover through the flavour of words the meaning
of a country she dimly remembered she'd once belonged in.

Francis Wilson

Turning Away

We turned away from the perfect curve
of the cove's white smile
and the candour of days on the beach,
the azures of skies and seas and days too much
to live up to; behind the rocks which ended it
was a kind of antidote: a secret mini-Utah
of furrowed cliffs, great men's profiles
and fossil faces, pitted and blind,
where water hauled about by the tides
was toil and regret tugging at the shore;
and just off-shore, by a taciturn rock,
a man, with his back to us and thigh-deep
in the swill, of kelp, of dead men's fingers,
of limey shells, of bloodless molluscs,
beside a small poor ancient boat,
was rummaging in its scuffed cuddy,
winding things and hauling them in, embroiled
in something urgent as if he wanted to hide
from us his mysterious purpose.
A genre scene: 'Fisherman at Low Tide' perhaps,
or a ghost, for there was a dark around him.
It shielded us from the bright day -
the unconvincing innocence of the beach;
the white smile, the 'azzurrissimo' (the brochures say)
that's difficult to stay untroubled in -
just for a moment: he retched the engine
into action suddenly; they reared up and out
bumping past a yacht, white logo of pleasure,
to keep his secret, his darkness, intact
far out, dark speck, half-swallowed by the glitter.

Judy Gahagan

Aso Rock and Two Elders

Three old men lie dozing on dreams,
rays of silk their robes,
our hopes their neckrest.
Merchants of power
pleasure
piety
(in that order of farming talent)
crouch
hunting
under shadows in three old men
sighing, chanting, counting hair on Divine beards
(in that order of human fecundity).
Chameleon clouds in
silvery cotton
dirty white
white of white
play sentry to
power
entertainment
ecstasy
their wings winnowing stars in heaven.
Watchful winds reap and sweep.
Knives in voices at Wuse Market and other numbers of Abuja.
Voices looking for three better dawns in three old men.

Okello Oculi

Uncle Aubrey

Uncle Aubrey is dying. On the line
pummelled by sheet-steel winds
night-clothes bluster and bulge.
Talk to him, cheer him up says Olwyn
so I tell him I have played on the moor
and seen hawks plucking at mice.
Hands pared to bone, he rubs knuckles
and remembers dead cousins
dead drunk at Christmas.
His head is too heavy for his neck
and his eyes yellow with sickness
too clotted to take me in.
He is dying in Welsh. It is part of me
singing somewhere in my blood
voices of sickness and rain.

Catherine Smith

The name of the bus

New times. My cousin plays golf with a black
government minister. The minister is relaxed.
Their kids share classes at the university.
In Khayalitsha, squatter shacks elbow for light.
Children with sparkling eyes go barefoot.
At roundabouts on Modderdam,
the grey-skinned youths they will become,
slouch, going nowhere. Parents hump carved giraffes,
masks, ashtrays to the City pavements; back at night.
And the bus, groaning and listing from its overload,
has words for it - a name, to carry to the centre
of glitz-fronted diamond-hearted Cape Town.
Imagine someone lashing out tight cash
on quality gloss paint, the kind to withstand weather,
bright green, electric orange; at least
two brushes: thick and fine. Then painting
the words for history, for the seeable future,
naming the bus, 'Suffering Continue'.

Carole Satyamurti

Green&Away

This year Green&Away has launched a conference-organising service using suitable halls for organisations seeking environmental and social change

Summer programme

20-23 August

A readers' weekend for *Resurgence* magazine, with speakers including Satish Kumar, Herbert Girardet, John Vidal and Walter and Dorothy Schwartz.

28-31 August

A long weekend of camping with a mixture of practical work and stimulating discussion on development work in Africa. Blacksmithing, tinsmithing, and tools refurbishing. A hive of lazy activity!

About us

Environmental organisations spanning food, Third World development, children and recycling will be meeting at Green&Away's unique outdoor conference site this summer. These all take place at a purpose-built centre with solar showers, electricity from the sun and wind, organic food and drink, in meeting spaces of coppiced hazel and recycled canvas.

'There is a definite need for environmentally-sound indoor and outdoor conferences', says Green& Away cp-ordinator Peter Lang. 'There is a clear need for environmental issues to be introduced to the conference world: delegates at far too many events listen to inspiring speakers urging them to protect the environment, and then troop out to a lunch of non-organic coffee, artificial creamer in plastic sachets and rooms with no daylight and a profligate use of electricity.'

For more info send an SAE stating which event you are interested in to:

Peter Lang, Green&Away, PO Box 40, Malvern, WR14 1YS

Mastering the history of slavery

Catherine Hall

Hugh Thomas, *The Slave Trade: The History of the Atlantic Slave Trade 1440-1870*, Picador, £25

Robin Blackburn, *The Making of New World Slavery: From the Baroque to the Modern 1492-1800*, Verso, £15

The similarity between these two books is limited to scale. Hugh (Lord) Thomas - known apparently by generations of students as 'huge tome', on account of his epic volumes on the Spanish Civil War, Cuba and the conquest of Mexico - has produced a 922 page book on the Atlantic Slave Trade. Robin Blackburn has followed his earlier volume on the overthrow of colonial slavery with over 600 packed pages on New World slavery. Both are synthetic works but here the comparison ends. The two books come from very different perspectives and provide many insights into the current contested state of history writing as well as the debates, both contemporary and historical, over the slave trade and slavery.

Hugh Thomas's epic has been welcomed with open arms by the right for it lays to rest, as they see it, the notion that the slave trade is all the fault of the West. It 'redresses the balance', restoring British self esteem in having been the first nation to abolish the slave trade. Bernie Grant, with his notions of reparation, can now be silenced with 'the truth': that truth is that Africans had established the slave trade long before Europeans became engaged with it. 'Magisterial', 'authoritative', 'magnificent' are some of the adjectives used to describe it. Writing in the *Mail on Sunday* (23/11/1997), Andrew Roberts triumphantly intones:

> Thomas likes big subjects. When he writes about the Spanish Civil War or the Conquest of Mexico, each in one vast, definitive volume, there is no need for another historian to return to it for at least four or five decades.

Such a notion of 'the definitive account' or 'truth' chimes well with Thomas's own notions as to what he is doing. He is not looking for villains, he assures us, as some historians do. 'The slave trade was, of course, an iniquity', he tells us in his introduction:

> All the same, every historian must recall Hugh Trevor-Roper's warning: 'every age has its own social context, its own climate, and takes it for granted ... To neglect it - to use terms like "rational", "superstitious", "progressive", "reactionary", as if only that was rational which obeyed our rules of reason, only that progressive which pointed to us - is worse than wrong: it is vulgar'.

To be vulgar, in Thomas's book, is worse than to be wrong. Take note, Bernie Grant! There is of course an important point here: that ideas have to be understood in their social context. But this is not advice that Thomas follows in his own work. This is a book about who did what and what happened, not about how those actions were thought about or understood. He continues,

> I would hate to be reproached for reading Alice in Wonderland because the author was a great-grandson of the slave trader Lutwidge of Whitehaven ... No one, surely, would refuse to take seriously John Locke, even as a philosopher of liberty, because he was a shareholder in the Royal African Company, whose initials, RAC, would be branded on so many black breasts in Africa during the last quarter of the seventeenth century ... I have tried in this book to say what happened. In seeking the truth, I have not thought it necessary to speak of outrage on every page... (p13)

The passage, with its implicit evocation of politically correct teachers stopping children from reading *Alice*, seems curiously out of date. Similarly, it is hard to summon up the imagined figure who would suggest that we should not take Locke seriously because of his associations with the Royal Afican Company. Again, the more likely response, and it is that of Robin Blackburn, is that we should take those associations very seriously indeed, and grasp the connections between Locke's ideas of private property in the metropolis and those of chattel slavery in the colonies. Thomas's conviction that he is simply going 'to say what happened' is also worth noting, for it assumes that it is possible to write 'the truth', having accumulated so many pages of facts. It appeals to the great British tradition of empirical history writing, which has been so undermined by post-structuralist critiques and Foucault's notion of the 'regimes of truth' which are established by particular relations of knowledge and power. Lord Thomas, it appears, remains unaffected by the turbulent storms which have racked so many historians in the last twenty years, and which have resulted in less authoritative claims to truth telling.

The Slave Trade tells the story of the Atlantic trade from its beginnings to its endings, and there is much that we can learn from it. Starting with the origins of the trade in the fifteenth century, Thomas traces the establishment of Portuguese interest in slave trading, growing out of sea faring activities off the coasts of West and North Africa. In Africa the Portuguese found a well-established trade in slaves which they were able to tap into. At first the slaves were taken to Portugal, but offshore islands, particularly Madeira, soon became the site of some of the first attempts to link sugar production with slavery. Portuguese and Spanish forays into the New World were soon followed by the involvement of other European powers and, by the eighteenth century, when the trade was at its most extensive, the British had established their dominance. At this point a section of the book deals with the trade itself, from the capture and sale of the slaves in Africa, across the Middle Passage to the New World. The high point of the trade marked the beginning of the end: the movement for abolition became increasingly significant in Britain and France by the end of the century, and the slave trade was abolished in Britain in 1806. The last section of the book deals with the attempts by Britain and the United States to police the seas and stop illegal trading, particularly to Brazil and Cuba, throughout most of the nineteenth century. While much of the book deals with well established patterns, it is important to have put these distinctive national stories together. The material on Brazil and Cuba is particularly welcome.

Thomas makes much of particular individuals and has telling vignettes of people and places. Julian Zulueta, for example, 'the last great slave trader of Cuba', a Basque born into a modest family, went to Cuba in the 1820s to work for an uncle who owned coffee farms. He became his uncle's heir, and further improved his fortunes by marrying the niece of his partner. That partner had an interest in slaves and Zulueta, with the help of his wife's money, was able to set up as a slave planter in the 1830s. He organised the journeys of the slaves, baptising and inoculating them before they left Africa, using steamboats and ensuring delivery to his own plantations. He was the originator of the scheme to bring Chinese labour into Cuba at a time of acute labour shortage, financed a railway, and established an office for the purchase and sale of slaves in New Orleans. He died one of the richest men in the Spanish Empire and a Marquis to boot. His name lives on in a street in Havana.

Much could be done with this story in terms of the gender order on which such trading depended, the place of science and religion in the organisation of the trade, the relation of the trade to capitalist accumulation, and the global nature of Zulueta's interests: unfortunately none of this is followed up, for Thomas believes it is individuals who are significant. Even at the individual level, however, such stories of the traders are unfortunately not matched with those of the men and women they enslaved. Equiano gets a mention but otherwise the exhaustive work which has been done to reconstruct slave narratives and culture goes by the board. Thomas's attitude to black scholarship is perhaps most vividly captured in his opening anecdote, when he recalls meeting Eric Williams, the Trinidadian historian and politician, at a dinner in London. Williams was shocked that Thomas had not read his work and instantly sent it to him. I was shocked that Thomas was not ashamed of his own ignorance.

Thomas's understandings of race provide me with my final note of discomfort about this book and its place in current debates. Thomas uncritically mobilises stereotypes of 'the African' which would seem simply old fashioned if we did not know how terrifyingly these stereotypes are reworked and utilised daily. The Atlantic slave trade lasted so long, he argues, because Africans could survive the heat and work hard, and because 'they were good-natured and usually docile' (p.793). He continues,

The most interesting aspect of the slave trade is that during the 500 years of constant contact between the Africans and the Europeans the former did not develop further in imitation of the latter. The reluctance of Africans to Europeanize themselves is often presented as a weakness. But it is more likely to be explained by some innate strength of the African personality which, however close the political or commercial relation with the foreigner, remains impervious to external influence (p797).

And finally, while slaves remain 'unknown warriors', 'the dignity, patience and gaiety of the African in the New World is the best of all memorials'. Magisterial indeed: Thomas's verdict on a continent and its people is unnerving.

Robin Blackburn's book is of a very different order, and is carefully placed within the best traditions of radical historiography with links to C. L. R. James, Eric Williams and many others. It is a powerful example of the best kind of self-consciously theorised history, aiming to modify classical Marxism's account of the place of slavery in capitalist development, and contribute to the current rethinking of the relation between slavery and modernity. It is a book which thinks big in terms of its comparative scope, and which is not afraid to offer a new grand narrative. Post-structuralist insights have inflected Blackburn's thinking but they have not put him substantially off-course.

Colonial slavery, Blackburn argues, was a hybrid of old and new, sacred and secular. He writes,

> Slavery in the New World was above all a hybrid mixing ancient and modern, European business and African husbandry, American and Eastern plants and processes, elements of traditional patrimonialism with up-to-date bookkeeping and individual ownership (p19).

Assembled from well-tried ingredients, the new slave systems were radically different in character from those that had gone before. While Roman slavery operated on a huge scale, it was tied first and foremost to the needs of the imperial state and paid no attention to ethnic origins. Slaves did an astonishing variety of kinds of labour, and were not held for generations into the condition of unfreedom. Colonial slavery, on the other hand, was throroughly commercial in character, it grew out of the new demand for tobacco, sugar and cotton, it came to focus exclusively on those of African descent and it was established as hereditary. While the great classical social theorists linked colonial slavery with tradition, backwardness and patrimonialism, Blackburn develops the arguments of thinkers such as Mintz, Bauman, Giddens and Gilroy, and explores the modern features of the system: its instrumental rationality, its association with the rise of national sentiments and the national state, its racialised perceptions of identity, its links with the spread of market relations and wage labour, its associations with the development of administrative bureaucracies and modern tax systems, and the growing sophistication of commerce and communication. The book is in two parts. The first is concerned with the emergence of a new slave trade and a new system of slavery in a Western Europe from which slavery had virtually disappeared by the fifteenth century. It traces the institutions and ideologies of that racial slavery, the establishment of the plantation as its characteristic form, with its first major testing site in Brazil, the struggle for survival between the early modern European states, the decline of Portugal and Spain and of the characterisic forms of state intervention associated with them, and the emergence of Britain, with its entrepreneurial merchants and traders fronting a dynamic civil society. While the Portuguese eye was always on the sea, the Spanish aimed to conquer huge tracts of land and turn their peoples into subjects. In Brazil, he suggests, the profits from sugar 'awakened the cupidity that had once focused only on silver and gold' (p183). The new meanings of plantation spread:

> By 1700 the word plantation, eclipsing previous meanings, now commonly referred to an overseas settlement producing a tropical cash crop, with tied labour, and by extension to an estate producing such crops, increasingly through the mobilization of black slaves (p309).

New racial ideologies spread too. Britain's 'Glorious Revolution' of 1688 confirmed an 'undisguised racial slavery' in the British Caribbean with a black skin as the marker of an inferior species, but with a system that depended for its workings upon the complex capacities of human beings. Indeed, Blackburn argues, it was the similarities between masters and their property which provoked racial fear. It was only too clear that slaves had the potential to resist and overthrow their masters, to sleep in their masters' beds:

> Fear and privilege, both constituted with reference to black slaves, possessed the ability spontaneously to 'interpellate' white people, making them see themselves as slaves might see them - that is as members of a ruling race - and thus to furnish them with core elements of their social identity(p323-4).

Race, a word which had carried meanings of family and kind, became a word denoting skin colour first and foremost. Slavery was detested in Europe as the condition of unfreedom, but was suited to Africans. Economic motives provided the key to the development of slavery for Blackburn, but racial ideologies developed in harness, and the reworking of given identities and creation of new social subjects was crucial to the success of the system.

The second part of Blackburn's book takes up the much disputed claims of Eric Williams that the profits of slavery were at the heart of industrial take-off in Britain, an argument which Thomas summarily dismisses as 'little more than a brilliant jeu d'esprit'. After a careful examination of the economic evidence, Blackburn concludes that, on the contrary, 'Exchanges with the slave plantations helped British capitalism to make a breakthrough to industrialisation and global hegemony ahead of its rivals'(p572). The plantations and the maritime enterprises which fed them marked an important intermediary form of economic rationality: the destructive and inhuman features of that system were a part of that modernity. Colonial slavery itself, in its baroque and creole moments, was an integral part of the transition to modern capitalism.

There is much that I have not discussed here, for Blackburn's is a rich and complex work. I particularly welcome its comparative grasp, both across the European nation states and across the different colonial sites of those states - from Ireland, to North America and the West Indies in the case of Britain. I welcome its recognition of the legacies of colonial slavery in the present, and the work that needs to be done in demonstrating this. I welcome its theoretical ambition and its attention to questions of cause and determination alongside its focus on social identities and racial ideologies. I regret the scant attention to gender, and the assumption that gender dynamics would never be motors of history. The makings of colonial masculinities were central, in my view, to the workings of colonial power, and the new racial order was always also a gendered order. I might want to argue with the primacy which is given to the economic, and claim that questions of cultural identity may, at certain conjuctures, have been the key factors of change. But this is a book to be worked on and with. Magisterial, I'd say.

Imagining Communities

Becky Hall and Susanna Rustin

Toni Morrison, *Paradise*, Chatto & Windus, £16.99

To a question from the floor about the possibility - or not - of a progressive separatist politics, African American novelist Toni Morrison responded with a playful glance around the auditorium. The occasion was a reading from her new novel, *Paradise*, at London's Logan Hall. Her answer, when it came, was a wry and inconclusive acknowledgement. 'That is the question,' she agreed with her questioner. And while it may be unanswerable, she suggested, yet it is a necessary one for the imagination.

Morrison is a captivating speaker and a mesmerising presence. Her audience was spellbound as she read from her novel. Paradise: a place rich with pleasure and devoid of conflict, an imagined community whose exclusivity is its guarantee of safety and goodness. Of course, she went on to explain, we crave similarity, the comfort of being among friends, part of a family, a nation or tribe. Paradise: a place peopled by the chosen, whose differences are erased in the act and the virtue of their admittance.

Yet any community imagined along these lines must live with its own negative image: the ex-community of the excluded, the disallowed, and the damned. The expulsion of this 'other' has always been central to Morrison's work, and the insistent complexity she brings to bear on questions of difference has marked her as a writer of unique sophistication. Refusing to invest in unproblematic versions of femininity or of blackness, Morrison's critical concern has been with the intersections between the discourses of racial and sexual politics. Her subjects, the characters in her fictions, are always constituted as sites of struggling identities, repressions and identifications. Neither blackness nor sisterhood is a cosy place in which to be. Rather, Morrison's political communities are riven by the conflicts and tensions produced by competing histories, memories and desires. The *Paradise* of this new novel, then, can never be the 'Haven' imagined by its founding fathers. As the narrative opens, with the massacre of five women, 'Bodacious black

Eves unredeemed by Mary', we prepare to witness the costs of their illusion.

Set in the 1960s and 1970s, the novel is about two communities and the relationship between them, in the period leading up to the murderous scene of 1976. Ruby is an isolated, all-black settlement in Oklahoma, founded at the end of the 1940s by a group of refugees from another black town, Haven. Less then thirty years old, Ruby contains a community struggling to exist by the principles of its own conception. The nine original families, 'Blackhorse, Morgan, Poole, Fleetwood, Beauchamp, Cato, Flood and both DuPres families' were '8-rock' people, 'blue-black people' named after the 'deep, deep level in the coal mines'.

The trauma of exclusion is the founding experience of this community, a jealously guarded and painful history which can bear no revisions. Deacon and Steward Morgan are the chief custodians of a past, a 'total memory' that is also their explanation:

> A story that explained why neither the founders of Haven nor their descendants could tolerate anybody but themselves. On the journey from Mississippi and two Louisiana parishes to Oklahoma, the one hundred and fifty-eight freedmen were unwelcome on each grain of soil from Yazoo to Fort Smith. Turned away by rich Choctaw and poor whites, chased by yard dogs, jeered at by camp prostitutes, they were nevertheless unprepared for the aggressive discouragement they received from Negro towns already being built.

Turned away from the emerging black towns on account of their midnight skin, the founders of Haven have passed on the burden of this devastating rejection to their descendants. Determined to defend against anything, 'inside or out', that threatens to rot 'the one black town worth all the pain', the Ruby elders clutch at the racial separatism that made their ancestors' 'dreamtown' a necessity. Seventeen miles outside Ruby lies the Convent, a community with strange histories of its own. The building itself was an 'embezzler's folly', taken over by nuns who turned it into a school for Native American girls. Having nursed the Catholic Mother, Mary Magna, to her death, Consolata, or Connie, is the sole survivor of this previous era. Under her care and a kind of supervision, the mansion now becomes an informal refuge for a disparate group of damaged young women - none of whom means to arrive, none of whom means to stay. Each woman brings her own, terrible story - broken, frightened girls, bearing ghosts and 'foolish babygirl wishes'. Mavis arrives in the green Cadillac in which her twin babies have suffocated; next comes Grace, or Gigi, searching for the rock formation of the loving black couple of Wish. Then Seneca, with the broken heart of a five year old child. Mavis and Gigi are rivals from the moment of their meeting: 'They did everything but slap each other, and finally they did that. What postponed the inevitable were loves forlorn and a very young girl in too tight clothes tapping on the screen door.' That girl is Pallas, aged sixteen, pregnant, and on the run from an unspeakable betrayal.

While personalities clash at the Convent, Ruby is bitterly divided along religious and generational lines. These conflicts are dramatically acted out at a series of public occasions. The principal source of political disagreement within the community centres around the wording on 'the Oven', the town's memorial to its founders, 'that both nourished them and monumentalized what they had done'. Its inscription, 'the furrow of his brow', worded by Zechariah Morgan, is invested with colossal significance, not least by Deacon Morgan, who takes a furiously conservative stand: 'Nobody, I mean nobody, is going to change the Oven or call it something strange. Nobody is going to mess with a thing our grandfathers built.'

Reverend Misner, Baptist leader of the town's largest congregation, is the spokesperson for the movement that wants to rewrite the Oven's inscription. A newcomer and outsider, Misner is allied with the young, whose desire to strengthen the command to 'Be the furrow of his brow' carries with it the determination of a new generation to address the town's past on its own terms, and to engage with a racial politics beyond Ruby.

Reverend Pulliam regards this suggestion with outrage: '"Beware the furrow of his brow." That's what it says clear as daylight. That's not a suggestion; that's an order!' Allied with the town's elders, Pulliam is a reactionary whose politics, like Misner's, are inextricably bound up with his religion: 'God's justice is His alone. How you going to be His instrument if you don't do what He says?' As the argument rages, the future of the Oven's inscription seems bound to divide the community, the symbol of its discontents.

History, then, is fiercely contested, its record the site of a desperate struggle. While Reverends Misner and Pulliam fight this battle as part of an ongoing religious war, the more secular perspective of historian Patricia Best, in the chapter that is named for her, provides the reader with a different and much needed context. Pat challenges Misner, questioning the direction of his leadership of the young:

> PB: 'Bible class? More like a war class. Kind of military, from what I hear.'
> RM: 'Militant, maybe, Not military.'
> PB: 'No budding Panthers?'

Pat's question refers us to the political world outside Ruby, articulating the connections between local government and the law outside. Her argument with Misner is an important reminder of the wider history in which the citizens of the town must play their part. More specifically, in her rejection of Misner's hunger for African origins, Pat draws our attention to the conflicts within Civil Rights. For while slavery, wars, and the ancestors' journey are all part of Ruby's story, its residents are conspicuously silent about the history of the present. The determination with which the town has barred its doors against the outside world means that the reader too is suspended in a kind of vacuum. In helping us to see past this barricade, Pat extends the scope of the novel's politics. What becomes clearer as the result of her critical intervention is that this community, and particularly its religious leaders, are reeling from the shock of King's murder, in a profound state of mourning for the land promised by his 'dream'. Shocked by the hostility of his enemy, Pulliam, Reverend Misner wonders:

> Had the times finally gotten to him? Was the desolation that rose after King's murder, a desolation that climbed like a tidal wave in slow motion, just now washing over him? Or was it the calamity of watching the drawn-out abasement of a noxious President? Had the long, unintelligible war infected him?... Was that the origin of this incipient hunger for violence?

While she props ajar the door to a grander American narrative, Pat is simultaneously absorbed in a much more personal 'history project', for she is writing her own version of the town's past. Begun as 'a gift to the citizens of Ruby - a collection of family trees', Patricia's research soon aroused the suspicions of her subjects: 'Parents complained about their children being asked to gossip, to divulge what could be private information, secrets, even.' Pat's work, and the resistance it meets with, are suggestive of the extent to which history is both ideological and subjective, for Pat is inextricably bound up in the history she is telling. At the nativity play, staged as a re-enactment of Ruby's own original journey, in which not one but seven holy families plead for shelter, Pat realises her exclusion from the select band of this official version. The revelation of her own 'Disallowing' comes as a profound shock, and she subsequently burns her papers.

Two generations of tragic love affairs have drawn Ruby men to the Convent, while women have gone there seeking medicines and refuge, 'barbecue sauce, good bread and the hottest peppers in the world'. When Soane Morgan invites the Convent women to the wedding of K.D. and Arnette, the two communities are far from strangers. A dynastic alliance of the Morgans and Fleetwoods, the marriage is designed to cement the traditional order, and ensure its continuation. What happens at the wedding, and afterwards, signals the beginning of a state of emergency. The crisis begins at the ceremony itself, at which Misner is bitterly attacked by Pulliam from the pulpit. It spreads to the reception, where the women from the Convent make a startling appearance and are chased off.

It is here, perhaps, that whispers begin to crystallise into murderous intent, for the spectacle of female depravity is provocation too much: 'None of them was dressed for a wedding. They piled out of the car, looking like go-go girls: pink shorts, skimpy tops, see-through skirts; painted eyes, no lipstick, obviously no underwear, no stockings. Jezebel's storehouse raided to decorate arms, earlobes, necks, ankles and even a nostril.' In their disgust at this brazen display of unrestrained feminine sexuality, the men of Ruby close ranks. Tolerable at a distance, the Convent has served as a useful site for fearful projections. Sexual promiscuity and pagan midwifery: abortions, miscarriages, and eventually all the misfortunes attendant upon the mysteries of reproduction, are blamed on the household of women. Named for the Morgan twins' dead sister, K.D.'s mother, Ruby is the virgin to the Convent's whore. It is the confrontation of the one with the other which draws the communities to the brink of disaster, the appearance of the women in the town which precipitates the final catastrophe: 'There were irreconcilable differences among the congregations in town, but members from all of them merged solidly on the necessity of this action: Do what you have to do. Neither the Convent nor the women in it can continue.'

It is left to the women of Ruby to intervene, or to defend their Convent Others, for while the town's religious schisms are momentarily displaced, the sense of common outrage and its vengeance takes a sharply masculine form. 'So,' thinks Lone DuPres, the elderly midwife who recognises the deadly nature of the fever by which the men are gripped, 'the fangs and the tail are somewhere else. Out yonder all slithery in a house full of women. Not women locked safely away from men; but worse, women who chose themselves for company, which is to say not a convent but a coven.'

As the novel revisits the moment of the massacre with which it began, it reveals one of its bitterest ironies. Cars parked at a safe distance, men with torches, guns and rope, the scene resembles nothing so closely as the lynchings of the Southern states their ancestors left behind. It is here, through this tragedy, that the descendants of Haven hope to reconstitute themselves as the 'New Fathers' of the town. Through this action, which mirrors the brutal persecutions and sectarian hatreds of the history they have tried so hard to exclude, they hope to recapture their untainted vision of a Paradise which is linked in imagination to a purer because less sexual femininity: 'God at their side, the men take aim. For Ruby.'

And there is magic at work. Lone's wisdom and Consolata's hands are touched with the powers of somewhere else. These are women whose pleasures and pains, comforts and skills, are both earthed and unearthly. The Convent women escape their private hauntings before the men arrive. Neither the Satanic refuge of the town's projections, nor the Christian sanctuary suggested by its given name, the Convent cellar is transformed into the stage for an unknown and unnameable ritual. The 'loud dreaming' whereby the women tell their stories begins a performance orchestrated by Consolata. Sharing 'half-tales and the never-dreamed', Mavis, Grace, Seneca and Pallas liberate themselves from the shackles of this world and the histories which bind them to it. It is perhaps this insistence on the presence of other worlds that leaves the reader so perplexed by the novel's difficult conclusion. Where or what is the beautiful place of Consolata's incomprehensible dream?...

> she told them of a place where white sidewalks met the sea and fish the color of plums swarm alongside children. She spoke of fruit that tasted the way

sapphires look and boys using rubies for dice. Of scented cathedrals made of gold where gods and goddesses sat in the pews with the congregation. Of carnations tall as trees. Dwarfs with diamonds for teeth. Snakes aroused by poetry and bells. Then she told them of a woman named by Piedade, who sang but never said a word.

It is hard to reconcile the mythical spirituality that consumes the Convent with the hope for a Paradise on earth; harder still to imagine how a timeless spiritual world might meet the agonies of history with the language of politics.

We must turn, then, to Ruby, where the people are busy rewriting the massacre. As the stories 'rapidly becoming gospel' compete for precedence, there seems little hope that the town will ever redefine the rigid boundaries of its Paradise. Yet the shrewd eyes of Pat Best seem to tell us otherwise. Gestures here and there, small and subtle shifts, suggest that the exorcism of the Convent women cannot restore Ruby to the 'New Haven' it once imagined itself to be.

We are left with the Convent women in their earthly bodies walking through the world, and competing versions of a biblical fantasy. Neither the damaged town, nor Reverend Misner's African time 'past the whole of Western history', nor Consolata's magical place can provide a satisfactory conclusion. Yet despite Morrison's hesitation about these narratives of redemption, she struggles to find another language in which to imagine an ending. While her hopes for another version of Paradise seem to rest with the Convent women, the constraining fantasy of the promised land means that the novel's concluding sentence is awkward, a clumsy yet suddenly necessary attempt to reconcile heaven with the possibilities of life on earth: 'Another ship, perhaps, but different, heading to port, crew and passengers, lost and saved, atremble, for they have been disconsolate for some time. Now they will rest before shouldering the endless work they were created to do down here in Paradise.'

Priceless?

Harriet Atkinson

Art Treasures of England: The Regional Collections
Exhibition at the Royal Academy of Art, January - April 1998

The explicit aim of the recent *Art Treasures of England* exhibition at the Royal Academy was to celebrate the wealth of the English regional galleries, and the richness of their collections. The agenda behind the exhibition was less celebratory than political - it was to highlight the increasingly poor financial situation of these galleries.

The show promised to bring together little-known masterpieces from all over England, never before seen in one place. This was mainly true; the works had never been seen together and were from far-flung parts of the country. However, there were disappointingly few works that were of outstanding quality. With the exception of drawings from Christchurch Picture Gallery, and a small number of paintings, there were few works that would have been considered 'masterpieces' by old school art historians.

On the other hand, some of the works on show, particularly those in the Victorian section, were well-known. For example, Yeames' *And When Did You Last See Your Father?*, with its depiction of a Royalist child questioned by Parliamentarian troops, is a familiar image. This, and other paintings such as Ford Madox Brown's *Work*, a visual polemic propounding the necessity of work and of education for all, are valued as visual histories or narratives rather than on aesthetic grounds.

As the exhibition showed, the non-London galleries are repositories of important Victorian paintings. This is logical: many of the galleries were supported by Victorian philanthropists who were buying works from the contemporary market for display within the institutions they had founded. A few of these galleries also have important works from the fourteenth, fifteenth and sixteenth centuries, but this is mainly due to the enlightened collecting policy of individuals like William Roscoe, who, as MP for Liverpool, bequeathed his private collection to the city.

There were almost no notable works from the twentieth century in the exhibition, only a number of less good works by important artists such as Bomberg, Wyndham Lewis, Freud and Gilbert and George. The inadequacy of these holdings showed up the reactive collecting policies of museum directors, who can only buy what is affordable or of local importance. If the exhibition can be regarded as a true reflection of the holdings of the 'regional' galleries rather than of the tastes of its curators (Giles Waterfield, Richard Verdi and others), the notable weaknesses in the 'regional' galleries were highlighted by the linear display. If the purpose of the show was to make the inadequacies of the galleries' collections more obvious, then it succeeded.

If the linear, art historical 'canon' was not deconstructed by the exhibition's curators, nor was any concept of 'regions' and 'regionalism'. In an interview, Giles Waterfield admitted that he and his co-curators had been banned from using the word 'provinces' or 'provincial' in connection with the exhibition. These words, he had been warned, had an implied derogatory meaning and so, he said, they preferred to call the collections 'regional'.

The definition of 'region' in this context was everything which was not in the capital. By delineating the boundaries of their exhibition in this way, the curators endorsed the very idea they wished to disprove. The problem of how to describe the non-London collections represented was admittedly a knotty one. However, if the words 'province' and 'provincial' have negative connotations, these are shared by the designations 'region' and 'regional', and the Royal Academy seemed to be importing works from the 'regions' to show London that the 'regions' aren't all that backward after all. Unwittingly, the curators cast themselves as explorers or discoverers who went out into the unknown vastness of the 'regions' to collect their plunder, and came back to London keen to display it. No meaningful dialogue between London and the 'regions' was initiated by this exercise.

The common ground for works within the exhibition was the fact that they are usually housed in the 'regions'. But this categorisation as regional meant that important differences between the collections were obscured. One difference, for example, is in the different financial contexts within which the institutions exist. Some are administered by universities, such as the Picture Gallery in Oxford University's affluent Christchurch College. Many others are part of museums services which continue to be under local authority control, while others are independent museums funded by the private sector.

The single factor which most of the contributing galleries have in common, apart from being outside London, is their poor financial situation. This was the real subject of and reason for the exhibition at the Royal Academy. The situation of local authority galleries has worsened in recent years as they have become increasingly marginalised within the structure of local government, easy targets for funding cuts. This is the ground which the RA, with well-publicised monetary difficulties of its own, shares with the 'regional' museums and galleries.

The exhibition did nothing to dissipate a further myth about funding: namely that these museums were all founded in ideal financial conditions, spawned by loving patrons, and sustained by happy councillors and art-hungry audiences. The first room in the exhibition paid tribute to the collectors and their galleries and gave the viewer a glimpse of the great men to whom we owe everything. This was a nostalgic's dream: if the context in which these museums were founded is examined, it becomes clear that they were set up at the whim of individuals or groups and could rarely have been effectively maintained. Birmingham City Museum and Art Gallery, founded as one of the central municipal services, alongside gas and water works and a library, and existing as such until the mid 1960s with the appropriate level of support, is a rare exception.

The pertinent issue which was forgotten by the exhibition is the changing context in which museums exist. The nineteenth century industrial cities no longer function as they did, and a belief in museums as temples of culture in which the lower classes can be enlightened and inspired is outmoded. This missionary motive has been replaced by a commitment to museums as a crucial leisure resource, as important preserves of otherwise defunct or forgotten histories. As such they are not the key feature of municipal architectonics which they once were, and it is not surprising that they are increasingly considered interesting but inessential.

The Royal Academy's show was interesting as an attempt to expose art lovers to a key issue in contemporary cultural debate: the funding crisis. It also tried to address the ways in which these collections can be sustained in the future. In this context, visitors were lured to the RA in the belief that they were in for a treat, and indeed, there were some treats in store. But more than this, visitors were invited to a demonstration of the poverty-stricken conditions of galleries outside London, and were offered the chance to reinvent themselves as a philanthropists.

The European Left

New beginnings for a European left

Martin Peterson

Approaches to multiculturalism

As the Millennium draws to a close, a surprising number of primitive groups seem to be flourishing in contemporary Europe - rough beasts slouching towards Bethlehem to be born again. Across the crisis-ridden Europe of the 1990s - whether in Leipzig or elsewhere in former eastern Germany, in Scandinavia, or in France and other Latin nations - public incidents of overt racism are disturbing the democratic process, and are draining time and energy away from progressive politics. Even where there are no major incidents of racism, there is the continuing attrition of everyday, low-level racist abuse. In current Swedish films and literature, there is a new absence of collective solidarity, especially among the working class, and this is represented as the stark reality of the 1990s. The fragmentation of daily life, and the aggressive racism experienced by minority citizens - on the way to work, at work and on the way home - are now a familiar theme of the new literary realism. This would have been inconceivable before the 1980s, and even in the 1980s there were few accounts of racism in Sweden.

In this context, right-wing parties have been able to exploit the political scuffles within and between the centre right and the centre left. A sordid example of this was seen in the recent French regional elections, where electoral opportunism took precedence over allying against the Front National. As a populist racist right, *Lepenism* is tolerated because it is believed that it is containable, and that it can be regarded as a buffer against the greater danger posed by violent extremists and fascist terrorists. Such a view is, however, a grave mistake. It must be properly realised that, wherever racism appears, democracy - now and in the future - is at risk. The existence of racism will always distort any progressive political programme or agenda for social justice.

After the political polarisation that took place within the pluralist democracies during the 1980s, European politics was brought back towards an incoherent centre during the 1990s, with calls for accountability and transparency. This has left the lines of ideological division unclear. An example of this lack of clarity is the diversity of popular scenarios outlined concerning work in the future - that is to say, the question of access to work or its absence. Some policy-makers have adopted somewhat coercive approaches, believing that the workless must be re-educated and made to accept whatever work may be available. In the politically volatile situation in Europe after the fall of the Berlin Wall, there was an opportunity for Europe's leftist parties to take new initiatives, thus enhancing their position. But this was not done. Instead, adjustments towards the political centre have remained the norm during the 1990s, and parliamentary parties in several countries have lost ground, in the face of initiatives taken by rapidly moving global capitalist interests.

A basic argument of this 'thematic bloc' of the centre is that, since cultural variations can no longer be subsumed in any grand emancipatory theory, any change-oriented democracy is exposed as fragile and existentially naked. This is amply demonstrated in two studies of the Swedish situation, which follow in this themed section. Alexandra Ålund analyses the shift in Sweden, away from a framework for multiculturalism, towards an increasingly segregated society, where racism has become virtually institutionalised. Ålund suggests that Swedish social processes may be veering out of control, in ways that have a significance beyond the experience of one country. Particularly powerful in her account is the inherent logic of this largely unnoticed - but almost total - change. Earlier, the virtuous cycles of economic growth, and belief in a larger theoretical perspective of social improvement, instilled people with hope and security. People in Sweden did not have much difficulty in managing social or economic problems, or the sensibilities of everyday social relations. Today, much has changed.

A second illustration of the relentless logic of a segregated society is given in Ove Sernhede's article. His protagonists, adolescents who are second generation immigrants, do not shy away from calling Sweden an apartheid society.[1] They are the victims of the erosion of the Swedish model, their futures trapped in the shallows and miseries of a drab and squalid suburban life. Like many other suburbs around Europe built during the 1960s and early 1970s, those built in Sweden stand out as being neither *Gemeinschaft* nor *Gesellschaft* (that is, roughly, offering the experience neither of solidaristic community nor of a diverse urban life). They are merely steeped in bleak concrete.

Elsewhere in Europe, these problems have been experienced for some time, and in some places small steps towards the recreation of society have begun to be put in train, for example in the rundown *Lyonnaise* suburb of Vénissieux, where there has been a refurbishment of old estates, and the creation of new housing projects.[2] In the Swedish case, unfortunately, the emergence of new class and ethnic constellations has coincided with the acute economic crisis of the 1990s. Clashes in the suburbs are not occurring solely because neo-fascist groups have located themselves in separate and somewhat segregated neighbouring communities.

As one way of coping with the new situation, the Swedish polity has opted to establish a new state agency, the Integration Agency. But the agency has immediately become the subject of public debate. Immigrant spokespeople, of varying political hues, have criticised it as serving to reinforce discrimination. And many people felt that the least the Social Democratic government could have done would have been to appoint someone with an immigrant background as its Director General.

---

1. In Sweden the term immigrant (*invandare*) is used to refer both to citizens of non-Swedish origin who have settled in Sweden, and to Swedish-born residents with at least one parent born abroad. In this article the translation of *invandare* has usually been 'immigrant', since it is not always clear whether or not those referred to are the first generation of settlers. In addition, the flavour of the article would have been altered by the substitution of terms such as 'ethnic minority' and other UK usages.
2. See John Pitts, 'Dickens and Flaubert: A tale of two housing estates', in *Soundings* 8, Spring 1998, pp125-146.

One crucial point concerns language. In the policy for immigrants developed in 1975, education in immigrant national languages - 'home languages' - was stressed as an integral part. It was assumed that the command of two or more languages would stimulate the mastering of any one language. Today the most powerful groups in the Swedish cultural establishment have put their weight behind campaigners who call for the use of only one language, Swedish, and who oppose multiculturalism.

This line is reminiscent of the remarks of the Vice-Chancellor of Uppsala University to a group of foreign students in exile in 1948, when he implied that they had better become Swedish, and learn to 'think Swedish', very fast - and that, above all, they should forget about their background. A quarter of century after this, the more enlightened multicultural policy programme was launched. Now, another quarter of century later, we seem to be back to square one. But this time there is an important difference: the Swedish polity and opinion-leading establishment today consists of people who are supposedly enlightened and vociferously anti-racist.

The language question has become symbolically decisive. It concerns a matter of political principle. Currently, Swedishness is perceived to be under threat, in the European Union. The Integration Agency is seen as one way of restoring the 'supremacy' of Swedish culture. Although these thorny issues of national and linguistic identity are now being faced by most nations in Europe, Sweden, because of its earlier progressive traditions, is perhaps the most striking of these cases.

From a different starting-point, but with a similar approach to what is essentially the same problem, Peter Weinreich, in his article, discusses the effects of the EU emphasis on 'welfare to work'. The Blairite workfare project, and the new work ethic which it encourages, is the salient instance. Weinreich foresees negative effects on ethnic relations in the UK, similar to those reported for Sweden. The 'workfare' instrument, he argues, defines exclusion solely in economic terms. Policies for social inclusiveness must embrace a much broader understanding of what produces a sense of belonging. The UK has, admittedly, come much further than most continental and Scandinavian nations in legislating and managing issues of ethnic cultural diversity. This is partly due to its longer experience; but it is also due to the sheer pragmatism of common law compared with the positivist laws of Germano-Scandinavia.

Weinreich's approach provides a perfect frame for Alexandra Ålund's argument. Weinreich expounds the 'Identity Structure Analysis' (ISA), which he has developed in the Northern Irish context of the University of Ulster. He has developed new qualitative methods for studying the psychology of cultural identities in multiethnic settings. This provides a powerful tool with which to illuminate the pitfalls and superficialities inherent in new labour market and educational training strategies. But Identity Structure Analysis also provides a viable basis for the eventual development of a multicultural constitution. Such a constitution is what the main theme of this issue points to. It is an absolute prerequisite of progressive politics from now onwards that a future welfare society be based on an elaborated and enlightened multicultural constitution.

Eastern Europe

What goes for Western Europe in this respect is just as relevant to Eastern Europe, different as it remains. This is amply demonstrated by Leonidas Donskis, whose Lithuanian background provides his point of departure. Few in the West have realised how archaic was the nationalism which played such a fundamental role in the initial transitional period in Eastern Europe after 1989. Still fewer have realised that this 'liberating' nationalism was, to a very large extent, brought into play intact from the more than sordid period of the late 1930s. Donskis looks at the realities of Lithuania, and clears away any undue ideological myth-making. For an Eastern European nation to acquire credibility, not only for itself but also in relation to the outside world (that is the West, or in particular the EU), it must divest itself of lingering chauvinist atavisms. It must show that it can face its current difficulties while supporting its ethnic and cultural minorities with a fervour equal to that which it bestows on its so-called nationals. At present, a forked tongue can too often be observed in public rhetoric - which may vary according to whether it is aimed at the EU, or is solely designed for domestic consumption.

The foremost indicator of progressive democracy on the move is the rise of social movements. Donskis shows that there already existed embryonic popular movements in Lithuania before the First World War. These now show signs of rebirth in the new conditions. The most promising sign, however, is that Lithuanian and Eastern European social demographies are changing, and with them value-formations are changing too.

Hungary is a more advanced but equally uneven nation. It shares the familiar Eastern European history of ethnic nationalism, visible from the time when modernisation and the ideology of the nation state began little more than a century ago. On the other hand, a form of 'civil society pragmatism' developed in Hungary, which was particularly marked immediately after the Second World War and after the 1956 uprising. The guiding principle of the Kádár regime - never to coerce but instead to cajole and persuade - created the conditions for the development of a practice of 'reciprocal exchange systems'. This was most visible in the reciprocal exchange of labour, which was widely used in rural areas where there was a notorious shortage of building workers. Reciprocal Exchange of Labour (REL) came to be used by households in many different situations, for a variety of purposes. And the vitality of social networks and traditions in contemporary Hungarian society has facilitated the survival of this institution. Máté Szabó is one of a number of academics who have analysed civil society and social movements in Hungary. In his article he analyses four major social movements, and their meaning and impact before and after 1989 - including the movements for civil rights, peace, the environment, and student protest movements. These, he considers, constitute a better indicator of the state of civil society and democracy than traditional social movements, or organisations representing particular interests, such as trade unions.

Szabó outlines the development of some of the new styles of associative politics which are occurring in Hungarian civil society. New youth organisations have emerged, or re-emerged, as have professional associations and artistic groups; in 1993 more than 12,000 groups were registered. As well as the National Federation of Hungarian Trade Unions, which is the continuation of the official trade unions of the former regime, there exist several major new trade unions. And symptomatically, as elsewhere in Eastern Europe, there are also a number of voluntary civil organisations and foundations that provide the main form of social care for the many newly poor.

In another perceptive study of a society in radical transition, Branka Likic-Brboric, in her piece on Slovenia, analyses features in Slovenian society which point to possible new political directions. Where others have observed a contradictory relationship between politics (the party state) and the 'second society' in Eastern Europe, she points to innovative elements in the Slovenian synthesis between the old and the new, which may have a wider validity. The prevalent situation in the new Eastern Europe has been that the political system has been gaining a relatively high degree of operative autonomy in relation to other societal spheres, and democratisation has implied the mere functional specialisation of politics, within a pluralist framework.

Branka Likic, along with other Slovenian analysts, argues that the growing operative autonomy of the political subsystem does not mean a separation of politics from 'society', but rather a radical change in the relationship between the political subsystem and its societal environment. This is a change that has taken place because the complexity of the political subsystem has been related to its growing capacity for self-reflection.

Other analysts have been less sanguine about the openings for a democratisation of the political system in Eastern Europe, and have been critical of the still-overwhelming control by the centre. But Branka Likic views the Slovenian experience during the 1990s in a more optimistic light. She sees as largely overcome the Eastern European 'dilemma of simultaneousness' (i.e. the problem of an absence of synchronisation between different spheres within society, which was part of the pattern of transition in Eastern Europe).

In this context, there is hope not only for an exchange of ideas between Eastern and Western Europe, but also for a cross-fertilisation. In the West, political, economic and social structures are much more rigid. Turbulence in the suburbs notwithstanding, the polity in each nation is clinging harder than ever to its existing system of domination. Thus it may turn out that the still pliable structures of Eastern Europe will provide experimental models for the whole of European society. However, it should at all times be borne in mind that multicultural constitutions must be a crucial part of any new settlements.

Left politics in the 1990s

Solidarity was a key concept in the aftermath of the Second World War: solidarity built the welfare state. But the concept of solidarity at that time was focused on very basic needs. Half a century later the level of aspirations is much higher. Society has become multicultural, and technically much more complex. It follows that the tasks of the left have also been raised to more demanding and sophisticated levels. It is no longer enough to think in terms of providing for people's basic needs, without considering the social context within which needs are met. There is a need to integrate the material and social dimensions.

This integrative form of thinking should not be confined to human needs: it is highly relevant to political systems too. For example, corruption in any one part may easily spread to an entire system. Thus it is worth taking note of the hopeful example of the South African Truth Commission. No analogous model has yet emerged in Europe, but painful self-purification through publicly-staged anti-corruption processes has been a recurring theme in the 1990s. Here the situation is full of contradictions. On the one hand, there is the necessity for containing corruption, but, on the other, merely ritual acts of purification - and these are an inherent feature of the current anti-corruption campaigns - can be harmful. It is very difficult to move forward politically through ritualisation, which may hide rather than resolve contradictions. In a similar way, to assert the complete separation of public and private spheres in no way furthers our understanding of new social possibilities.

In order to get a proper perspective on the current impasse we need to go back two decades. The despondency felt by many in the 1970s expressed itself in an extended intolerance; this was a symptom of a depressive reaction to the failure of the heady days of the 1960s to topple a single regime. But few noticed a fundamental and positive change that did actually occur in western democracies during the 1970s. Public rhetoric began to assume an increasingly anti-authoritarian tone, which encouraged a radical attitude towards outdated hierarchical structures. Progress also occurred in the sphere of working life, and at local and regional levels, again on the basis of a healthy mistrust of power.

As well as reforms in industrial relations, experiments were made in decentralising decision-making, for example in France, Italy, and Sweden - and current plans for devolution in the United Kingdom fit into this pattern. The intention, or effect, of such initiatives was first to broaden democracy and then to make it more responsive to social change.

This meant that, as the 1980s approached, each of the three actors of neocorporate tripartism - business, labour, and the state - was ready to accept a furthering of the democratic process, and, indeed, a fundamental breakthrough for democracy was envisaged within industry and other hierarchical institutions. It was predicted that the last bastions were about to fall, even in serious studies from noted business schools on the American East Coast. With hindsight we know that as soon as 1980 arrived, the opposite of all this took place. The business community had been pragmatic enough to make use of the radical rhetoric for its own purposes. And it monopolised the concept of 'flexibility', a gift from the left: the left was effectively disarmed and overrun using some of its own methods. Throughout the 1980s the left continued to score further own goals, most glaringly by declaring that it was the political right that was raising all the pertinent questions.

The 1980s can be seen, paradoxically, as a Proudhonian revolution instigated entirely by the interests of capital. Indeed, the decade was one of many contradictions, and this aided the legitimation of rationalisations in industry, and a double focus on the local and the global. As a result it began to seem as if the nation state was being squeezed out (though it now seems that its resilience was underestimated). As the nation state continued to be central to the political strategy of the 1970s, the slightest indication of its vulnerability, or even its future demise, was very destabilising.

The deregulation of capital flows carried out during the 1980s provided for a radically new kind of financial speculation, and only those most experienced in the ways of markets could master this game. Meanwhile traditional issues of the left became marginalised, while previously neglected issues, such as regionalism, and new ones, such as the democratisation of Eastern Europe, became a fresh source of political diversion. Hence there was hardly any questioning of the complexities of the electronic revolution, which on the one hand bolstered the rationalisation of industry and led to lay-offs and redundancies, and on the other hand made possible the flexibility, inherent in neo-Proudhonism, that finally promised to rid industrial society of both Fordism and Taylorism.

Actually some features of this neo-Proudhonism were already evident during the 1970s. Moreover much of the huge investment in electronic technologies that took place during this decade was not fully recorded in economic statistics, and this gave out the wrong political signals. This lack of information gave rise to misleading ideas about the potential for a democratic breakthrough during the 1980s. Under the cover of the necessity for deregulation, which social democrats everywhere subscribed to, a new process of concentration of economic power took place, instead of the promised economic democracy. The 'big bang' at the London Stock Exchange heralded a new age of hedge-funds and derivatives, beyond the reach and influence of political institutions. This has contributed to the gradual decline in the credibility of the political class across Europe.

For the adventurous and to risk-takers the 1980s offered economic rather than political stakes. Individual contracts offered by employers, and quality circles on the shop floor, reduced the power of the trade unions. Also significant were the socialist initiated *groupes d'expression* or open dialogue between the parties in industry. These new measures added up, perhaps unintentionally, or maybe through lack of political imagination, to the institution of a new corporate culture, which came to replace the political initiatives of the 1970s.

In the mid-1970s the currently very successful Danish social democratic finance minister, Mogens Lykketoft, when presenting a summing up of the Danish and the Swedish wage earners' fund experiments, wrote as follows:

> In the Scandinavian debate on wage earners' influence, profit-sharing in the US is frequently cited as an example of how not to democratize production ownership. It is pointed out that the numerous, unorganised small shareholders in large American corporations make it easier for a few shareholders to control a great amount of capital while owning only a very modest percentage of the shares. 'Wage earners' funds' would prevent a similar situation from occurring in Scandinavia. [3]

Unfortunately, what Lykketoft warned against became reality in the 1980s. Wage earners' funds were eventually only half-heartedly tested, before being scrapped. 3.5 million Swedes, or 40 per cent of the entire population, are today shareholders. Most of them hold shares in collective funds, but a growing number have acquired shares as part of a wage bonus. The influence of the shareholders is minimal, owing to the exceptionally strong concentration of ownership of capital that has taken place during the recent decade.

It was collective capital formation during the 1950s and 1960s which paved

---

3. M. Lykketoft, 'Toward Economic Democracy', in John Logue and Martin Peterson (eds), 'Special Issue on Industrial Democracy', *Scandinavian Review*, No 2, 1977.

the way for the major infrastructural achievements which transformed housing standards and the transport system in much of Western Europe. Today a similar collective investment could go into the formation of co-operative firms and environmental enterprises. If they had been allowed to acquire shares freely in the 1960s, as the Swedish Confederation of Labour (LO) wanted, pension funds could have contributed to a much higher yield, and thereby saved these funds from their present prospect of being heavily depleted by 2020. In addition participation by the pension funds could have rescued the small- and middle-sized enterprises in Sweden from the near-oblivion that they suffered during the crucial years of recession, around 1990.

D eregulation, and the free movement of capital, have delivered a gigantic shift of power to those groups who have capital to move. This has also changed the measures by which standards of well-being are judged in individual nations. Not so long ago the important parameters were the rate of employment, economic growth and real wages, indicators of health, education, and the status of women. Today nations are ranked according to budget deficits, inflation or currency values. These indicators demonstrate very clearly where mobile capital should go. That is their purpose. Hence governments are adjusting their capital and property taxes to the level of those nations with the lowest rates of taxation. All over Europe the share of state income which is derived from company and capital taxation has fallen substantially during the past decade. Tax amnesties are pervasive. In Sweden, formerly the 'old model' of social democracy, the rate of company taxation, at 28 per cent, is now among the lowest in the western world.

Those groups who do not have any capital to move around have had to bear the brunt. Swedish housing costs are now the highest in Europe. Previously the housing market was regulated and the average costs of housing amounted to only 19 per cent of private consumption, whereas today they are well over 30 per cent. The state raised taxes on housing by 60 per cent between 1995 and 1997, but not for the purpose of redistribution. The burden of taxation has in practice been laid upon the poor, in order to ease the movement of capital for the rich. It is an urgent priority of the broad leftist front to find a way out of this impasse. To this end, familiar slogans and the magic of old rallying concepts are no longer relevant. The primary goal must be the winning-over to such a front of the large group of individualist small entrepreneurs with basically petit bourgeois values.

However, the mere conception of any broad leftist front, or broad church as the Labour Party called it in its seemingly moribund stage during the early 1980s, has no sense or content without a guarantee of multicultural democracy. A necessary basis for democratic action is the absence of segregation, exclusion and tensions in the suburbs. In several articles in this section of *Soundings* it is testified that these are elements which not only obscure the prospect of democracy but divert attention from the important issues of radical politics. Increasingly, internal security and the closure of national borders are being launched as a necessary counter to globalism.

In earlier days, we relied on collective organisations, which had credible, overarching and progressive ideologies, to push anachronisms such as ethnic conflicts onto the scrapheap of history. It seemed easier then both to understand and guide the advance of democracy. For lack of a written multicultural constitution, new multicultural societies such as Sweden, Holland, Denmark and Germany, are currently experiencing cultural and ethnic turmoil. Without such a multicultural settlement, the modern equivalent perhaps of the class settlement of the post-war period, the entrepreneurial endeavours of those from various ethnic backgrounds will not flourish. Nor in these circumstances can there be a revival of any semblance of a welfare state. Conversely, if multicultural constitutions were to exist in European nations, there would be every chance of the development of a broad leftist front which could encompass radical liberals from Central and Eastern Europe as well as the leftist interests which lost influence at the time of the formation of their societies in the early 1980s.

The European left initiatives of the 1970s ended in disenchantment. And the end of the Cold War dissolved many illusions about the state of socialism in Western as well as Eastern Europe. While socialism in Eastern Europe appeared to have made people lose faith in politics in general, leftist ideology which drew on notion of a simulated universality in Western Europe was also appearing quite moth-eaten. However, there is still a positive array of leftist institutions to build on. These include targeted social networks, the concepts of both human and social capital, and the existence of huge collective funds - topics which are briefly explored in my final article.

The debate does not, in fact, have to be begun once more from scratch.

There are new social movements in formation, in different parts of Europe, for example in Italy.[4] The establishment of strong social networks for the promotion of an informal economy is another positive development. This tendency is to be seen both in Sweden and France, two nations where innovative ideas have frequently advanced the leftist cause. In his article in this section John Crowley gives an analytical introduction to the intricacies and current implications of the French version of a welfare state. He shows how ambiguity has complicated its development. Some long-standing and tenacious French institutions are currently severely at risk because of the effects of global processes. Alain Caillé follows Crowley's analysis in his acute comments on recent trends in social movements in France, and on a leftist alternative to the present Jospin government. He points out that its limits of action are becoming evident despite a national and a regional election victory.

Examples of new Swedish perspectives provide further food for thought. Sweden has gone through so many turbulent swings during the past dozen years or so that moments of self-reflection have become both numerous and shattering. The transformation of the former Swedish model began in the early 1980s. It was as late as 1982 that the last fundamental law of the social state (the 'Social Service Act') was enacted in Sweden. By 1983 the collective front of the trade unions, the basis of the so-called solidaristic wage policy, began to crack, as the metal workers refused any longer to restrain wage claims.

Wage earner funds were a source of many problems. Deregulation, and most importantly the end of currency controls, came swiftly and shook the system profoundly. The competence to manage these changes was simply not available to the Social Democrats. Dreadful mistakes were made by both public and private flagship institutions. Sweden was thus landed with unemployment figures that were among the worst in Europe; in the OECD's economic league table Sweden fell to 18th place, with only the poorest Mediterranean nations below; there was a new poverty, shared among broad layers of the population irrespective of qualifications such as had not been seen since the 1930s; and new antagonisms tore deep wounds in the social fabric. A recent comparative survey on poverty in Europe has reported that as many as one third of the households in Gothenburg are presently on or below

---

4. This will be the subject of an article in a future issue of *Soundings*.

the poverty line.

New, informal, but vociferous, oppositions from within the old labour movement have emerged, expressing considerable rage. On May Day celebrations during the past few years, new oppositional groups have been more impressive than the formal labour representation - the Social Democratic Party and the national labour federation. Under these circumstances new political constellations and approaches are being called for. Not least, it is now beginning to dawn upon the polity that the multicultural issue will be decisive during the next few years. In this respect, Sweden may fulfil a symbolic role once again, if it can advance a first attempt at a multicultural constitution.

Slovenia
A model synthesis

Branka Likic-Brboric

The dissolution of Yugoslavia has developed into a contemporary tragedy of gigantic proportions. In the eyes of world opinion, the civil war and ethnic cleansing taking place in, above all, Bosnia, Croatia and Kosovo have not only brought social progress to an abrupt halt but have turned it sharply backwards. Out of this debris the previously relatively unknown but highly sophisticated Yugoslavian debate on ideological and social evolution has been brought to a wider European forum. This article by Branka Likic-Brboric is a brilliant reflection of this debate, and it suggests ways of developing new leftist approaches in new democracies base on the Slovenian example.

Yugoslavia: an aborted modernity project

The development strategy of the Socialist Federal Republic of Yugoslavia was initially regarded as a success. The economic achievements of this reductionist modernisation model, which was based on industrialisation as a panacea, led to various forms of differentiation. The legitimacy of the system was based on the alleged solution of both national and class problems. This model, which today forms the backbone of the Milosevic regime in Serbia, has regularly been challenged by calls for modernisation. The patriarchal power structure described by the Yugoslav League of Communists was incisively questioned by not only the student movement and the Praxis philosophers, but also by influential liberal-managerial groups within the republics and among the Federal political establishment (who had developed and thrived on the social and economic basis of Yugoslav decentralised workers' self-management and market oriented reforms). Similarly, the legitimacy of the central administration was questioned by the ethno-nationalist movements that often sprang forth from factions within the communist organisations at the republican level.

Several institutional changes took place during 1965-75. These resulted in the transfer of decision-making processes to regional levels, which became manifest through the Constitution of 1974. Already in 1969 the Croatian educational system had oriented itself in a direction of its own. In 1976 the Associated Labour Act curtailed the power of management with the effect that the design of a contractual socialist economy was set forth. These changes, though intended to enhance economic efficiency through workers' self-management and to raise governmental legitimacy and meet democratic demands through self-government, instead provided regional leaders with the opportunity to forge independent power bases and exercise a pervasive bureaucratic control over the economy. This intensified inter-regional competition for already scarce resources. Furthermore, the Yugoslav 'debt trap' caused economic pressures which resulted in re-peripheralisation, a process of re-bureaucratisation and the re-traditonalisation of society at the level of the republics, which became dominated by local bureaucracies without any grandiose visions of internationalism.

Yugoslavia was a rent-based nested hierarchy of patron-client linkages in which the institutional divisions - between state and market and between politics and economics - required for a market-based society did not work; and ethnic violence was the result of ill-considered market reforms and the general political drift (which was a consequencence of 'neo-classical nostrums') - trends such as the curtailment of demand and the elimination of governmental regulation and control of the economy.

In the long and uneven process of reform to a market economy (the tensions between ideals and reality led to a lowering of democratic aspirations under pressure from market rules and forces) the failure to meet the plethora of historical and political visions brought about by the dynamic forces of modernity unleashed the economic, political, social and moral crises of the 1980s. Hence political elites felt obliged to proceed to more fundamental reforms such as property rights' reforms. The rhetoric and ideology of workers' self-management was duly replaced by the rhetoric and ideology of the free market and efficiency. The top-down, authoritarian programme was overtaken by a variety of informal socio-economic and socio-cultural institutions that were determined by regional survival strategies.

The austerity measures imposed by the last Yugoslav government increased foreign exchange reserves to eight billion dollars, while the Dinar remained convertible and inflation was curbed. While the earlier inter-republican conflicts were triggered by the uneven distribution of foreign loans, market shares and rents, new divisions arose which were more concerned with the distribution of the costs of economic reform. In the former case common survival strategies among political leaders meant that conflicts could be managed whereas in the current case no such consensus was evident. Protectionist economic policies replaced joint decision-making. The consequences were a reduction in mutual trade, increased levels of ethnic mobilisation, and eventually the violent disintegration of Yuogoslavia.

Competing visions

The failure of the Yugoslav modernisation project may have been due to the cultures, ideologies and practices of the political elites having been cultivated in separate historical and geopolitical contexts. Such a paradox as unemployment in a socialist economy could then be explained by pointing out the existence of competing visions of the state (the Slovene model and the Foca model) in spite of common development and reform strategies.

The Slovene model of administration and economic strategy was long characterised by an effective governmental apparatus, a tradition of local self-government, civilian control of all economic affairs, and a commitment to national liberalisation whose origins can be traced to Austro-Marxist influences. The Central Committee of the Communist Party of Yugoslavia established governing rules, in line with Slovene ideas, that were based on sound economic principles, cooperation, and self-governance. However, their application in a region destroyed by the Second World War, where the army competed with the poor for supplies, implied the use of different means, namely, 'persuasion, rather than a money price'. It is these different means which determine the nature of the Foca model.

Even though differing regional combinations of these two extremes can be identified within the territories of the former Yugoslavia, it is the idea of a decentralised state that strongly distinguishes Slovenian political traditions from those in Croatia, Serbia, and Bosnia, which are basically authoritarian and self-enforcing.

The Republic of Bosnia-Herzegovina, marked by a particularly stubborn merger of neo-Stalinism and a traditional patriarchalism, stands out as the typical example of the Foca model. The experience of Bosnia-Herzegovina also epitomises the debacle and institutional void in post-socialist countries that is the result of the dogmatic application of the shock therapy model. As an alternative to post-modern ethnic deconstructivism it was wholly inappropriate. The economic crisis of the 1980s reaffirmed patterns of domination and patriarchal bureaucratic practices disguised in the robes of particular national interests.

Urban civil society did not utilise the brief period of 'democratic' pandemonium before nationalistic parties won the elections to instill their values or to devise a realistic path of political and economic reconstruction. The external forces of post-modernism, traditionalism, and a neo-conservatism led intellectuals and the media alike into a spider's web spun by political elites and populist movements in a search for easy economic spoils, that had no clear political or democratic vision. This state of affairs was mirrored in the resulting devastation of human, material, and moral resources. But even without a war it would have been difficult to reverse these negative trends. Measures imposed by various stabilisation programmes during the 1980s had caused a grave deterioration in the economy of Bosnia-Herzegovina while simultaneously undermining both the social position of the middle classes as well as their influence on the political process.

Today, following the Dayton Accords, the World Bank's reconstruction programme offers no substitute for the plethora of conflicting historical visions and national political programmes that have had such a devastating effect. There is a need in the former Yugoslavia for a 'strategic framework for reconstruction, reform and economic management' (UNDP).

'Creative destruction': the Slovenian experience reconsidered

If it is at all possible against the background of the 'destructive destruction' of Bosnia-Herzegovina to speak of a Schumpeterian 'creative destruction', then it is useful to analyse the Slovenian model, which stands out as one of the most promising among the formerly socialist countries in transition.

Slovenia is usually considered to be a strong and successful reformer, this in spite of the high transition costs caused by the loss of markets and resources through secession and long and exhausting debates regarding the choice of privatisation model. For this reason, it is valuable for other economies in transition to explore whether her 'success' can be ascribed to the external factors determined by her favourable geopolitical position, or whether it depends on political vision, internal expertise, experience, and other historical, cultural, and ideological advantages. Furthermore (due to the challenging competitiveness of the Japanese firm and the pressures of globalisation), workers' management and participation is still a very interesting subject at the level of organisational studies in the search for a more efficient form of organisation. Because of the civil unrest in former Yugoslavia it is possible to assess and follow the transformation of this Slovenian model within a long term perspective.

The Slovenian path of development

Due to the powerlessness of the Kingdom of Yugoslavia in solving regional disputes, because it had inherited a strong industrial base and a pool of industrialised workers and a corresponding level of socio-economic development, Slovenia initially held a privileged position in the Second Yugoslavia. In addition, the anti-centralist and liberal orientation of her political leadership placed Slovenia in the leading role in the Yugoslav pursuit of a more efficient economic organisation. The institutionalisation of the ideas of workers' self-management and socialist self-government were particularly crucial in this respect.

Slovenian Prime Minister Stane Kavcic (removed from office in 1972) was the first major Yugoslav political leader to be devoted to economic efficiency, market solutions, decentralisation, and support for initiatives aimed at forging closer economic ties with Western Europe. He advocated the 'shareholders model' of self-management. Similarly, certain Slovenian social and economic thinkers emerged as the primary critics of 'social ownership' as 'non-property', in that neither the state nor the workers' collectives were owners or responsible subjects and that managers were merely executive organs of workers' collectives. Consequently, managers' powers were not curtailed as much in Slovenia as elsewhere during the 1974-76 so-called 'anti-technocratic' reforms, and the views of financial experts were valued more, since the managers were recruited mainly from industry. This is in contrast to Serbia or Bosnia-Herzegovina, where managers were less interested in production or design because they were primarily politicians. It was thus not by accident that the most efficient firms were located in Slovenia, and that no gigantic, politically determined, and eventually failed investment projects were assigned to Slovenia. All the other republics had at least one such symbol of political megalomania.

Slovenia left behind the perils of the dissolution of Yugoslavia without totally falling back onto pre-socialist political practices; rather it built upon the structures and relatively positive experience acquired through the operation of a decentralised economy based on social property, self-management, and partial reliance on the market mechanism. In the early 1990s the Slovenian population comprised just 8.5 per cent of Yugoslavia, but they produced 20 per cent of the Yugoslav GNP, 30 per cent of overall exports and held a 12 per cent share of the external debt. The rate of unemployment was at the same time well below the average. While Slovenia's real GDP plunged by 22 per cent during 1987-91, her per capita income and economic structure (primary sector 5.6 per cent, secondary sector 42.8 per cent, third sector 51.6 per cent) clearly placed Slovenia on a par with other post-industrial nations.

The early path from a command to a market economy taken by Yugoslavia served the Slovenian socio-economic development well. Slovenia had moved beyond a shortage economy and its economic position stood comparison with the other ex-socialist countries. Bearing all this in mind, it is not surprising that foreign expert advice was not taken at face value. Indeed, all three ingredients of the standard approach, namely, macroeconomic stabilisation, liberalisation and privatisation, were called into question.

Macroeconomic stabilisation

The DEMOS coalition won Slovenia's first multi-party elections in April 1990 with the new government being formed a month later. One of the first items on its agenda was the preparation of a macroeconomic programme, including both fiscal and monetary reform. Macroeconomic management had been relatively successful, especially considering Slovenia's initially very low official foreign exchange reserves and the lack of external financial support. The role of foreign experts in these processes was viewed as, and continues to be, controversial. Joze Mencinger, the former deputy prime minister, argues that Slovenia's success has been due to the fact that its internal Slovene policy-makers did not fully implement the stabilisation programme proposed by the foreign experts, Sachs and Associates. Contrary to their recommendation that a nominal exchange rate and a nominal wage be introduced, thus pegging the new currency to the German mark and the ECU, or a basket of currencies, a rapid conversion of Dinars to the new currency and a floating exchange rate were pursued in line with the advice of Slovene economists.

However, Slovenia also experienced a typical transformation crisis, with a cumulative fall in GDP of 14.5 per cent in 1991-92 and an increase in unemployment to 14.4 per cent in 1993-1994. This negative trend began to be reversed in 1993, but seems to have become possible only after the resolution, through long and exhausting debates, of the issue of the privatisation of state enterprises, a matter which, according to Joze Mencinger, 'caused major dissent within government, divided politicians and had become the root of political instability'.

The privatisation debates

Because of the obvious need both to revise federal laws and to develop Republican legislation concerning privatisation, the DEMOS government prepared the first draft of a privatisation law, known as the Korze-Mencinger-Simoneti code, in November 1990. This was approved on an initial reading by all three chambers of the Slovenian Parliament for further legislative consideration. (In the old Slovenian constitution the Assembly consisted of the Socio-Political Chamber, the Chamber of Communes or Municipalities and the Chamber of Associated Labour - the latter comprising representatives of the various branches and organisations of the economy who were elected by working people; the three chambers reviewed and approved of legislative proposals in a three-step procedure.) This new law envisaged a 'gradual, decentralised and commercial' privatisation, a conception that was partly a revision of the federal law adapted to Slovenian circumstances. These included the relative independence of enterprises, the regional dispersion of industry, the existing industrial structure, close links with foreign firms, the financial means of the population (an estimated US$ 2.5 billion was held in foreign banks or 'under mattresses' and an additional US$ 1.2 billion was frozen within the banking system), and the old Slovenian contention that economic ownership, particularly the role of management, should be strengthened.

'Slovenia has been successful partly because its policy-makers did not fully implement the foreign experts' stabilisation programme'

Accordingly, the Government's function was to be restricted to defining the rules of privatisation and supervising their implementation through the Privatisation Agency and the Development Fund, the latter making assistance available to large loss-makers. Although there was to be no free distribution of property, certain discounts to citizens and employees were allowed for. Firms were also supposed to initiate privatisations in which managers, workers, citizens, and both foreign and domestic legal buyers could participate. Particular importance was given to leveraged management/employee buyouts that resembled American Employee Stock Ownership Plans (ESOPs).

Although all three chambers passed the draft law at the end of March 1991, the Privatisation Law itself was blocked by criticism from both left and right and was never brought to a vote. While the Slovenian labour unions demanded the free transfer of more than one third of a firm's value to both active and retired employees, the former (pre-Second World War) owners claimed full compensation for their previously nationalised companies, including lost profits. The right wing of the DEMOS coalition brought anti-Communist rhetoric into the critique of the proposed law and prepared an alternative proposal, the Sachs-Peterle-Umek code. Both Joze Mencinger, Deputy Prime Minister for the Economy, and Marko Kranjec, Minister of Finance, resigned in May 1991, soon after Jeffrey Sachs visited the Assembly in order to promote his well-known idea of centralised, mass, and distributive privatisation (which was presented as the final draft of the previous privatisation proposal).

Sachs envisaged the nationalisation and conversion of large enterprises into joint stock companies while the smallest enterprises would be able to privatise spontaneously. Also proposed was the method of free distribution of shares to all citizens through financial intermediaries such as banks, pension funds, and mutual investment funds, also controlled by government officials. The Yugoslav Federal Army withdrew from Slovenia in July 1991, after the short war, and the new constitution was decided. It was a troublesome autumn for the Peterle government as his privatisation proposal was criticised by organised managers, trade unions, economists, and government officials alike. Peterle, a Christian Democrat, disregarded both Slovenian liberal political traditions as well as the legacy of the national circle of professional economists in the search for active and responsible owners.

Even though Slovenia was officially recognised by the EC on 15 January 1992, and then in April of the same year by the US, 'the window of opportunity' for the government had closed, the DEMOS coalition split, and Peterle was forced to resign after a no confidence vote. J. Drnovsek, the liberal Prime Minister of the new government installed in April 1992, showed a will and ability to compromise, thus allowing for a co-operative political framework inclusive enough for many different interest groups to articulate their positions. The Law on Ownership of Socially Owned Companies, passed on 11 November 1992, and amended during the course of 1993, was a centrist solution, containing elements of decentralisation and gradualism on the one hand and distribution of ownership certificates to all citizens on the other. By the terms of this law, 40 per cent of social capital would be transferred to public funds: 10 per cent to the Restitution Fund, 10 per cent to the Pension Fund, and 20 per cent to the Development Fund, of which one fifth would be freely distributed to all Slovenian citizens in accordance with their age. The employees would be entitled to free distribution of a further 20 per cent of social capital through shares in their enterprises.

Although actual privatisation started slowly, it was completed at the end of 1997 for all 1545 eligible enterprises.[1] Among the various methods utilised in the process of ownership transformation, the most common have become 'the internal buyout' of shares and the mandatory transfer of 40 per cent of shares to institutional owners. In general, managers and employees hold a maximum

---

1. OECD, *Economic Survey of Slovenia*, Paris 1997, p92.

of 60 per cent equity in 78 per cent of privatised companies, while holding a majority in more than 85 per cent.

Nonetheless, restructuring costs have been considerable. By the middle of 1992, approximately 98 large companies with aggregate losses of over DM 1 billion and employing almost 10 per cent of the labour force were transferred to the Development Fund and around 50 per cent of managers were replaced in the period 1990-1992. The unemployment rate has remained high, young and old workers and ethnic minorities being the main losers, but the position of women has improved with restructuring towards the financial sector both in terms of female/male wage differentials, which were relatively high even before transition (.88 in 1987 and .90 in 1991), as well as in terms of a lower probability to become unemployed. This may be attributable to the fact that the Slovenian government did not blindly follow the neo-liberal transition recipe.[2]

Transitional strategy in Slovenia

As consensus on the issue of privatisation was being reached, Slovenian business people, professionals, and politicians came to adopt the position that the government should take a more active strategic role in order to facilitate transition and ultimately integrate Slovenia into the EC. A strategic industrial approach was advocated in order to enhance production efficiency since research had shown that Slovenian productivity was 2-3 times lower than that of Western competitors. The protection of national interests was emphasised insofar as this strategy did not rely on a crucial role for foreign direct investment (FDI), even though a liberal legal framework for it had been set up.

The emerging Slovenian economic system appears to be a mixture of the German bank system with its workers' participation, the American stock market with its investment funds and bankruptcy rules, and the Japanese model of informal networks. But the particular results of the privatisation process in fact conform to a marked degree to 'the legacies of self-management and dispersed decision-making'. It is important to emphasise the remarkable pragmatism and inventiveness of Slovenia in respect to the official introduction of a system of co-determination similar to the one in Germany,

2. *European Forum for Democracy and Solidarity*, Brussels 1995, p27.

in addition to the fact that the introduction of a system of profit-sharing is being considered by many firms.

The continuity in path-dependent change should not of course be overstated, given that workers' self-management was transformed into management over workers in line with the overall privatisation shift from politico-ideological workers' participation to management-centred employee involvement. Nevertheless, the Slovenian experience appears to follow a heterodox institutionalist frame of reference, which suggests how the legacies of the past and the perceived international economic and political realities may be moulded together within a political process to define a viable economic system and a successful strategy for transition. In the particular case of Slovenia one can discern the positive role played by a modern co-operative and pragmatic political culture, which was the product of a path-dependent process of cultural and communicative modernisation defining an effective democracy, which both inspired and continually reshaped top-down reform and transition recipes throughout the history of the Second Yugoslavia.

Conclusions

This story of Slovenia's transition does not imply that the typical economic problems and social tensions related to the application of the standard recipe were avoided. Nevertheless, adjustments to the particular domestic circumstances were necessary in order 'not to kill the patient'. Slovenian experts had recognised early on, and discursively promoted, a model similar to the above-described contingency approach that was oriented towards integration into the EU based on centrist ideologies. Furthermore, both formal and informal political institutions, along with the dominant political vision, have proven to be sufficiently inclusive and transparent to offer a broad framework in order to comply with the many different interests that have been articulated in the long process of defining the legal framework for privatisation. Finally, foreign experts have perceived this approach as a country-specific, non-ideological, and practical model of transition which is a stimulating alternative to shock therapy.

However, the delay in Slovenia's full integration into the EU and NATO may be related to new initiatives for the regionalisation of the Balkans, which have been greatly influenced by external political and economic pressures. Slovenia might probably have to supplement its original transitional strategy and national policy - which was aimed at mediating international competitive pressures through public governance - with efforts to participate in the process of development of new forms of cooperation in the region of the Balkans. This at present unpopular redefinition of the strategy may provide dividends in the long run in light of the very small size of the Slovenian market. Despite its relatively successful transition experience, Slovenia in 1998 has not yet returned to pre-transition levels of industrial production, and pressures from product markets and further liberalisation are expected to intensify.[3] On the other hand, the consciousness of the potential contribution of a focussing upon social capital is at the same time expected to provide Slovenia with the instruments to steer on a new course.

A longer and slightly different version of this text will be published in C-U Schierup (ed.) Scramble for the Balkans: Nationalism, Globalism, and the Political Economy of Reconstruction, *Macmillan Press, forthcoming.*

---

3. EIPF, *Gospodarska Gibanja*, May 1997.

New social movements in Hungary

Máté Szabó

Máté Szabó assesses the development of Hungary through analysing the fortunes of social movements prior to, and immediately after, the democratic elections of 1990.

Background

Hungary's contemporary history follows a general East European pattern in terms of its successive waves of social movements. In the early nineteenth century, liberalism and nationalism mobilised the Hungarian middle strata; and then after the revolution of 15 March 1848 and the independence struggles against the Austrian emperor, a compromise between the Austrian and Hungarian aristocracies in 1871 gave way to modernisation, the development of a market economy, urbanisation, and industrialisation. These social processes mobilised blue collar workers, the urban proletariat and the peasantry at the end of the nineteenth century, in the socialist movement. This followed the patterns of German-Austrian social democracy in its fight for the extension of electoral rights and social security. Agrarian socialism was strong, as it was in Southern Europe. At the end the First World War, in 1918, a short-lived radical liberal revolution severed links with the Austro-Hungarian monarchy, followed by the Communist coup d'etat in 1919 which was defeated by foreign intervention. In the interwar period, the authoritarian regime of Horthy suppressed both left and right radicalism, but the alliance with Nazi Germany encouraged the mobilisation of Hungarian fascism, so-called 'Hungarism'. After the Second World War, a short-lived democratic period ended in the Communist takeover. The Communist regime dissolved and suppressed all autonomous traditions of social movements, liberal, socialist and fascist as well. Under this regime, all real social movements of civil society were suppressed, and 'pseudo-movements' were created. These were huge, bureaucratic government- and party-led organisations calling themselves social movements, and adopting the form of trade unions, peace movements, patriotic fronts, etc.

This situation led to a 'freezing' of social mobilisations, except during the period of the anti-Stalinist revolution in 1956. However, a prolonged period of government terror, together with the demobilisation of civil society, followed this tragic event. Unlike in Poland, there were no autonomous mass mobilisations in Hungary before the Gorbachev era. To understand the development of social movements and protest in present-day Hungary, one needs to go back to the mobilisations before 1989, and during the transformation period. Thus the first part of this article provides a short overview of the former oppositional, 'underground' movements against the Kádár regime. The second part then considers how mobilisations around these issues are faring in the new Hungary.

The transition 1986-1989
Civil rights movements

In Hungary, as in other former communist countries, informal networks of intellectuals, clustered in small groups, protested against the suppression of civil rights. Since the 1970s their protests have ranged from subscription campaigns supporting civil right demands, the spreading of information on the state of civil rights, to informal discussions and gatherings. The institutionalisation of civil rights under a democratic, pluralist system alters the form of civic activity. Within an institutionalised political process, the 'catacomb' forms of suppressed and persecuted political subcultures are transformed into formal organisations. In the first free elections in Hungary after communist rule, in 1990, two liberal parties succeeded in obtaining parliamentary seats in the opposition ranks. Both of these developed from suppressed socio-political movements of the Kádár era into influential political parties of the new Hungarian democracy. The Alliance of the Free Democrats (Szabad Demokraták Szövetsége, SZDSZ) and the

Alliance of the Young Democrats (Fiatal Demokraták Szövetsége, FIDESZ) are both products of the institutionalisation of anti-communist protest movements which demanded civil rights and democratisation. At the leadership of both parties are former civil rights activists.

The student movement

There is in Hungary a long political tradition of social movements organised within the framework of student hostels. The protest of students played an important role in the post-communist transition. One of their important networks was the nation-wide network of self-governing student hostels. In the first period of Hungarian democracy after 1989 there were new developments in the self-governing student hostels movement. Once FIDESZ as an organised political party left the student milieu, the students and especially the hostels network became depoliticised, and ceased to play their former 'avant-garde' role in political protests. The political activism of students had played an active role in the crisis of the Kádár regime. They had built up informal networks, organised conferences on politically 'forbidden' subjects, published *samizdat* periodicals, and established co-operation with civil rights activists and the 'ecopax' movements.

Peace and antimilitarism

In the Kádár era, unofficial peace initiatives like the 'Dialogue-Circle' challenged the Moscow-oriented foreign policy of Hungary, so harsh repression was used to suppress them during the 1980s. The international networking with Western European, and with similar Eastern European peace movements, was especially hindered and punished. The supporters and organisations of conscientious objectors, seen as 'enemies of the state', were tried and sentenced by the courts, and politically persecuted. Nor did the Catholic hierarchy, which seemed to be broadly on the government side in this conflict, support them.

Ecology and environment

Ecology movements played a central role in the protest against the late Kádár regime during the second half of the 1980s. Their dynamics were built on the protest against the construction of a joint Hungarian-Czechoslovak dam on the Danube (the Duna). The protest against construction of the dam mobilised broad support - it was criticised as the last dinosaur or 'Dunasaur', that is as a last monster project held to be polluting, destructive, non-profitable and typical of gigantic socialist industrialisation. Under pressure from mass protesters, in 1989 the last communist government stopped the construction of the dam.

Despite the absence of an organisation of national unity against communist rule, such as Poland's Solidarity, protest issues were important in the Hungarian transformation to democracy. The biggest popular mobilisations took place on 23 October 1988 (and 1989), this being the anniversary of the Hungarian revolution of 1956, and on 16 June 1989, to commemorate the reinterment and rehabilition of the 1956 revolutionary leader, Imre Nagy. In August 1988 there was an anti-Ceaucescu demonstration, and on 15 March 1989 the anniversary of the Hungarian national and democratic revolution of 1848 was celebrated. During these events, when tens of thousands rallied on Budapest's streets, joint action of relevant oppositional groups could be established, and the divisions between more nationalistic or democratic tendencies were put aside in the common cause of the anti-communist struggle. However, during the Round Table talks in the summer of 1989, the unity of oppositional groups was dissolved. The first divisive issue to emerge was whether to accept or reject a strong presidential leadership, that is whether or not to follow the Polish pattern. Radical liberal democrats organised a successful plebiscite against the bargain made by the populists, and in October 1989 nationalists and reform communists, who both supported a strong and directly elected presidency, were defeated.

Protest movements after 1989

At the beginning of 1989, a law on demonstrations was passed (A gyülekezési jogról, 1989/III). From this time onwards, the political elite of the Communist Party was no longer able to pick and choose between different protest groups and demands, tolerating or rejecting them according to the views of the dominant political factions. The framework for organising demonstrations in Hungary became normatively regulated. The police now have only a restricted jurisdiction to reject some applications, on the grounds of the risk of disproportionate disturbance to traffic, maintaining public order, and securing the functioning of parliament and courts where demonstrations are held near to their sittings. But there is recourse to a judicial review of such decisions of the police, at short notice. Police action is thus meant to secure public order and not to restrict the freedom of gathering and expression. From this point of view, the practice and problems of policing mass demonstrations in Hungary are more similar to those in Western democracies.

During the 1990 electoral campaign, the Hungarian oppositional movements became actors in the fragmented party system. Electoral campaigning was already going on during the conflicts about the presidency, and adversarial political behaviour emerged among the nationalist, liberal and socialist political camps, all divided or fragmented in a plurality of political parties. The parties divided and differentiated themselves around rather symbolic or culturally oriented issues, whilst the real situation was dominated by an underlying consensus on the market economy, on a pro-Western orientation in foreign relations, and on political pluralism.

How then did the former suppressed oppositional movements fit into the new institutional structure?

Civil rights

Of course, conflicts and problems related to the issues of civil rights are also apparent in the new Hungarian democracy. Many liberal- and socialist-minded initiatives were established during the 1990-1994 period against the Christian Democratic government's policies. New protest organisations arose to fill this new space. These included: the Democratic Charter - an umbrella organisation of civil rights movements; the Raoul Wallenberg Association (Wallenberg was a Swedish diplomat who rescued Jews from the Holocaust, and himself disappeared in a Soviet concentration camp); the Martin Luther King Association; Action Against Racism; and the Club of Publicity, devoted to particular issues in the defence of civil rights. These new initiatives were organised in the framework of political pluralism, either without any or with only indirect links to former anti-communist protest movements. Their absence of an 'underground' past makes them similar to Western movements. Whilst the former 'oppositional' groups of the communist period have been institutionalised as political parties of the post-communist system, new issues have led to the growth of new groups, linked to national and international networks.

Students

The fact that the former student opposition movement, FIDESZ, became a normal, 'adult', political party left a space for student activism, in which different youth and student political organisations are now competing. The law on higher education in 1991 banned all politically- or ideologically- based student organisations and movements from the system of self-government, apart from HÖK. Based on the (West) German university model, the 'students' self-government' (Hallgatói Önkormányzat, HÖK) has the legal monopoly of representation of students' interests within the universities. Making the most

'Paradoxically success against the Duna dam led to a demobilisation of green activists'

of its monopoly of interest-representation, HÖK has moved towards abandoning the relatively autonomous self-governing student hostels.

Student movements are now separate from political parties and self-government, so they tend to be rather apolitical. They are economic, welfare, or culture and life-style oriented. Student protests during the 'first legislature' period of Hungarian democracy - the waves of 1992-1993 and 1995-1996 - were oriented towards higher education-specific demands, against the introduction of fees, and rejecting cuts in welfare services for students. Student protests no longer integrate both broad political demands and the specific goals of youth, student autonomy and self-government. In the transformation of higher education in Hungary there are new conflicts which raise transitory student protests. But these do not articulate general political demands, as did their predecessors in the communist system. They seem to be oriented, like the recent student protests in the West, largely towards the problems and discourses of the higher education system itself.

Peace and antimilitarism

After democratisation, new types of antimilitarist movements emerged: the Alba Circle, the League of Antimilitarists, and the Alternative Network. These were established to protest against all forms of violence, and to support conscientious objection. While they refer back to the traditions of the unofficial peace movements of the 1980s, there are few personal continuities, those that do exist being mainly among the religious groups protesting against military service. The new peace movements were organised under the new, pluralist political conditions. Their issue-orientation follows the changing patterns of international politics. They are now concerned with general issues of antimilitarism rather than the bipolar system of mutual deterrence. The popularity of this position has often been linked with the particular issue of the war in the former Yugoslavia, and later with Hungary's plans to join NATO. Since 'alternative' military service was institutionalised during the democratisation of 1989-1990, it is only radical religious groups who continue to campaign for an end to all forms of military service. More important for the majority is the development of new legal opportunities, as well as providing help for conscientious objectors, and to individuals who choose alternative non-military service.

There is stable but small-scale support for the actions of these groups. Despite the solidarity and active help of intellectuals, these remain undercurrents of the Hungarian protest culture. Only if the peace and antimilitarist protests combine with the civil rights campaigns of 'Democratic Charter', or the non-violence of 'Campaign Against Hating' - a coalition of protest organisations - might it be possible to organise mass protests. The solely antimilitarist or peace demonstrations and campaigns remain concerns of youth, student, intellectual or religious subcultures alone. In 1997 communists, radical nationalists and peace activists opposed the first moves of Hungary towards joining NATO, but there was no joint action among the three pillars of this ultimately weak campaign.

Ecology and environmentalism

The withdrawal of Hungarian support for the Danube dam project in 1989, and the subsequent cessation of construction on its side of the river, led to a simmering conflict between the Hungarian and Slovak governments, on which the International Court of the Hague gave its first judgement in 1997. Owing to the fact that the governments during this period, 1990-1997, had more-or-less accepted the demands of the protest movements, the concerns of Hungarian environmentalists became somewhat redundant. Paradoxically, their success in preventing the completion of the dam led to a demobilisation of green activists. Since then, the actions of ecologists have become oriented more towards regional issues rather than being focused around the direction of energy policy in Hungary. Previously, environmental groups, like all unofficial movements in the communist system, were forced to articulate demands for civil rights, under the pressures of a restrictive political control. The introduction of a constitution and the adherence to a rule of law has led to environmentalism becoming increasingly professionalised. The ecology movement has maintained its protest movement character in Hungary by concentrating on 'specialist' ecology issues. It is no longer concerned with political issues, such as calling for a change of regime, or the introduction of civil rights into the constitution, as it was formerly.

There have been attempts, in Hungary, to organise green parties according to the model seen in Austria and Germany, despite the absence of any inclusive, nationwide, causes. Around the time of the elections, in 1990, there was division in the green movement between traditional environmentalists, and alternative ecologists. This opposition was paralleled by the earlier conflict between 'official environmentalists' and 'underground ecologists'. The Green Party was from the beginning paralysed by these conflicts, and had an unsuccessful electoral campaign. Well known environmentalists and ecologists, distributed across the political spectrum, tended not to become involved in the internal debates of the Greens. The disharmony in the Green camp was such that, as an organised political party in 1994, they were unable to present themselves as the legitimate representative of the Hungarian ecology movements. This allowed a since disbanded 'Ecofascist' party to gain in popularity, a development which horrified the public.

Despite their unsuccessful foray into party politics, Hungary's ecology movements are doing well. By means of networks and initiatives, the environmentalists formed themselves into a high profile protest movement with real influence. Supporters are drawn from numerous regional and special issue-based movements in order to participate in 'Earth Days', or at annual meetings. Ecology movements are able to mobilise mass support on some issues - like the protest against the Mohovce atomic power plant in Slovakia – formed by a coalition of politicians from across the party spectrum. An analysis of press reports of protest events between 1989 and 1995 showed that for each year about 10 per cent of all protests originate in the 'green camp'.

Following the Hague ruling in 1997, the issue of the Hungarian-Slovakian dam was revived and led to the Socialist-led Hungarian government trying to make a deal with the Slovaks. In the knowledge that any agreement between the governments could lead finally to the construction of the dam, the green networks are once more mobilising mass demonstrations and petitions. They have succeeding in convincing the smaller coalition partner of the Socialists, the Liberal SZDSZ, to break with the government's seeming compliance with Slovak demands. March 1998 saw the Hungarian government refuse to concede to the proposals of the Slovaks, who are currently trying to initiate a new hearing of the case at The Hague. Though the issue looks far from settled, the green protest inspired another partial victory.

Outlook: prospects for the new millennium?

As we have seen, the mobilisation of new social movements, which occurred in Western Europe during the 1960s and 1970s, was mirrored in Hungary both during and after the fall of the communist regime. Activism and protest became an integral part of civic culture in the post-1989 period. Hungary's closer links with the European Union should result in a further convergence with the social and economic processes of Western Europe. For the counterparts of western NGOs in Hungary, the process of Europeanisation may lead to them gaining more support than they have hitherto enjoyed. But continued integration will also generate new social and economic conflicts. The new social movements may have the capacity to increase bargaining power and 'veto-potential' within civil society. Such new social activities may mark the end of the old and pave the way for a democratic Hungary in the new millennium. The 'participatory revolution' may help to produce a market economy and pluralism 'with a human face'.

Soundings

Soundings is a journal of politics and culture. It is a forum for ideas which aims to explore the problems of the present and the possibilities for a future politics and society. Its intent is to encourage innovation and dialogue in progressive thought. Half of each issue is devoted to debating a particular theme: topics in the pipeline include: Windrush Echoes and The Concept of Care.

Why not subscribe?
Make sure of your copy

Subscription rates 1998/9 (3 issues)

INDIVIDUAL SUBSCRIPTIONS: UK - £35.00   *Rest of the World - £45.00*

INSTITUTIONAL SUBSCRIPTIONS   UK - £70.00   *Rest of the World - £80.00*

Please send me one year's subscription starting with Issue Number _____

I enclose payment of £ _____

I wish to become a supporting subscriber and enclose a donation of £ _____

I enclose total payment of £ _____

Name _____

Address _____

_____

_____ Postcode _____

Please return this form with cheque or money order payable to Soundings and send to:

Soundings, c/o Lawrence & Wishart, 99A Wallis Road, London E9 5LN

Reconciling past and present in Lithuania

The future of radical Lithuanian democracy

Leonidas Donskis

Recognised as one of the most brilliant scholars of the new generation of Lithuanians, Leonidas Donskis provides a perspective on the painful process which a new eastern European nation must undergo in order to adapt itself to an increasingly global setting. The situation demands that it create not only a transparent political system but also a radical civil society capable of social innovation. Donskis is better placed than most to interpret the historical and cultural obstacles to modernisation which are inherent in new eastern European societies.

Twentieth century Lithuania manifests itself as one of the specifically central European phenomena in history. It cherishes its memory and reputation as one of the multi-ethnic, multi-religious and multi-cultural models of Renaissance Europe. At the same time it has been transfigured into a typical homogenous actor of contemporary history. Already in inter-war Lithuania the 'one nation, one language, one culture, one state' principle had become predominant. This principle both then and today has been recognised as a prerequisite for democratic reform movements not only in the Baltic States and Eastern Europe but universally.

Nationalism is the key concept of modern Lithuanian emancipation. At the same time the older historical ideal of a multi-cultural Lithuania, which once made it legendary, meets the criteria for a progressive contemporary European democracy. Is it possible to reconcile, within the framework of the current nation state's institutional settings and discursive practices, the ideals of both nationalism and multi-culturalism? Where within this dichotomy does Lithuania lie today? If Lithuania, as well as the other Baltic nations, remains at the nationalist pole, how will they reconcile democratic ideals with those of an increasingly multi-cultural Europe? How does a small-state Eastern European nationalism relate to civil society? To what extent can this nationalism be inclusive and liberal?

Moral cultures and progressive nationalism

Throughout history, civil society was the main frame and agent for the radicalisation of society. It implied the keeping alive of progressive elements under the duress of oppression, and an opening-up to greater tolerance and democracy. In short, modernity, in the central/east European context, depended upon the state of civil society. So it does today.

One of the basic conditions of modernity is the emergence of what has been referred to by Ernest Gellner as human modularity. The Gellnerian metaphor of modular man sheds new light on the kinship between civil society and nationalism. Like a shared egalitarian culture in the age of nationalism, human modularity is a phenomenon of social mobility and widespread literacy. Ironically and paradoxically, both civil/liberal society and nationalism are the offspring of human modularity. By releasing the human flexibility and connectiveness that are so important for civil society, modularity at the same time comes to forge a specific consciousness and culture. Nationalism rests on nothing but the making of a shared culture and of its objects of common devotion. Within this limited scope certain democratic ideals may be refined, but nationalism provides too narrow a frame to enable progressive ideals to thrive.

The root thinking of Eastern Europe is illuminated by Louis Dumont's explanation of the origins of the Herderian philosophy of history and culture as an extension of cultural individualism. Herder, as Dumont suggested, developed from the political individuals of French and British philosophy, the idea of a sort of collective individual, notably the nation, which was historically unique and self-sufficient, and had the same rights of self-determination as human individuals.

A glance at the history of the past century confirms how widespread this sort of collective cultural individualism actually was in central Europe. This, the German variant of modern ideology, is deeply grounded in central and east European political culture. In the early phase liberalism and nationalism were both compatible and complementary phenomena. Liberal nationalism was a familiar element, but in due course these paths diverged. In the Lithuanian context this process has been best contextualised by Vytautas Kavolis, the pre-eminent émigré sociologist who died in 1996.

In Kavolis's interpretation, liberalism and nationalism were not only compatible but bridged individual and collective identities. This Lithuanian liberal nationalism in fact had an impact on the movement of Bulgarian democrats. But since nationalism was the essential ideological feature in the modernisation and national emancipation of Lithuania, its reinterpretation during 'the springtime of the peoples' manifested itself in the visions of Adam Mickiewicz and Giuseppe Mazzini and in the popular national struggles for independence. This meant that the radical progressive part of nationalism was lost, while populist nationalism deteriorated into an ethnic-and-linguistic-cleansing nationalism. Kavolis called this a moral provincialism that got increasingly massified, doctrinal and ideological. Its later success in, for instance, Romania was symptomatic of the political culture prevailing there. Because of the impact of social Darwinism on the thinking of the new polities in east central Europe and Lithuania in particular, nationalism was reshaped within quite a narrow frame of the exclusive ('zoological') defence of people's interests by any means.

However, the historical virtue of once having been a prototype of the multi-ethnic, multi-religious and multi-cultural state fascinated Kavolis. Being aware of how problematic the search for the origins of radical liberalism would be in east central European political history, Kavolis tried to identify both the particular liberal stances and the element of social radicalism in Lithuania's national rebirth. Kavolis had a qualified view of the *Ausra* (Dawn) and the *Varpas* (Bell) initiated respectively in 1893 and 1897. These were secularised social movements, whose effect was to establish a sharp dividing line between the progressive movements offered by liberal nationalism and the politics of conservative nationalism. Kavolis was, however, unique in Lithuanian culture in his attempts to provide a theoretical framework both for the polylogue of moral cultures and for the reconciliation of progressive liberalism to an inclusive nationalism that was expected to leave room for the embrace of the Other. This interpretation enables us to recognise that progressive movements today can only be given life through the revival of cultural liberalism.

Lithuanian nationalism and subsequent popular proactive and reactive movements made linguistic-cultural affinity the principal element of sociopolitical cohesion. These currents then became the basis of institutionalised politics after 1918, ending up as the authoritarian regimes of the interwar period as conservative nationalism became the mainstream of nationalist identity politics. Thus it must be noted that there is an ideological kinship between present-day social movements and the forerunners *Ausra* and *Varpas* of a century ago.

However, the most conspicuous and trend-setting contemporary social movement was *Sajudis* (1988), which virtually repeated in its own way the sequence and logic of the earlier transfigurations of Lithuanian nationalism. Having started as the upholder of the 'for our and your freedom' principle, inherent in the ethics of radical liberal nationalism, and having contributed to the struggle for human rights, civil society and civic-mindedness in the former USSR, *Sajudis* ended up as the collective defender of 'Lithuanianness' and Lithuanian 'spirituality', in the face of imagined threats both from within and from without, such as the sinister KGB network, clandestine international organisations, and the threat of Western cosmopolitanism and mass culture in general.

It must never be forgotten that the nationalist intelligentsia has played the decisive role, in central and eastern Europe, not only in the nation-building process and the emergence of new political entities, but in the theoretical and ideological definition of nations and their cultures as well. 'Lithuanianness' and its identity formula was tantamount to being Roman Catholic. Conversely, according to this implied identity hierarchy, Roman Catholics were perceived as the exponents of true Lithuanianness, whilst lesser creeds followed at some distance. Whereas ethnic minorities were earlier simply excluded from the category of Lithuanianness, post-Soviet times offered a new lip service to tolerance. However, to be liberal and agnostic represented the true radical stance between these two authoritarian systems.

The national philosopher Antanas Maceina embodied the prevailing inter-war authoritarianism by opting for both Nazism *and* Bolshevism. This stance epitomised mainstream nationalism at the time. In a both surprising and sinister way Maceina's ideological idioms are still alive and well as models in present-day Lithuania. There are calls for restrictions on the activities of Poles, Russians and Jews to freely express their views. But there is also, fortunately, a generation gap in the outlook of the different social movements of Lithuania. Young Lithuanian intellectuals prefer to relate themselves to historical times marked by multi-culturalism, such as those of Renaissance and Baroque Lithuania. This familiar invention of a political and cultural tradition is perceived of as an alternative to the dominant political discourse. There is no reason to deceive anybody by glorifying the Polish-Lithuanian Commonwealth as any model of pluralism, but this search among the new generation for a way to combine the past with contemporary global realities is symptomatic. This rediscovery of the beginnings of religious and political tolerance in the sixteenth century Polish-Lithuanian Commonwealth, and of its multi-cultural nature, calls for new definitions of the terms 'nation' and 'culture', which the new generation feels have become worn-out and exhausted, deconceptualised and overgrown with ethnocentric myths and superstititon. Paradoxically, the rejuvenation of the collective consciousness, which leads the efforts of young historians to theoretically reconstruct and reveal not only Lithuanian but also non-Lithuanian (i.e. Polish, Jewish, Russian, etc.) Lithuania, may be much more useful than all of Lithuania's new sociology and political science centres put together.

The young historians are now liberating themselves from the myth of the nation, and its definition, creation and defence, that is still cultivated by the dominant literary and academic establishment. The younger historians see this nationalist model as inapplicable to their field of study. The same goes for other young humanists, who are longing for multi-dimensional ways of looking at history and culture.

Realities in the 1990s

Since 1990 Lithuanian political culture has demonstrated a new political willingness and ability to accommodate and contextualise minorities, their languages and cultures. Unlike in ethnically and hence politically divided Latvia and Estonia, where social peace and civic solidarity remain less predictable, Lithuanian mainstream politics has succeeded in embracing, or at least not alienating, the Russian, the Ukrainian and the Belorussian minorities. Lithuania has even become a shelter against censorship and political persecution in neighbouring lands. The existence of small groups such as Karaites and Roma is not causing conflicts.

Things are more complicated with regard to the Jewish and Polish minorities. The problem for Lithuanian Jews is that quite a large segment of society - including not a few representatives of the Lithuanian intelligentsia - is still inclined to treat them as collectively responsible for the Soviet occupation on the eve of the Second World War. There still exists a notorious theory of the historic guilt of the Jews for Lithuania's disaster. Lithuania has failed to bring war criminals to justice and finally to provide an unambiguous legal assessment of those Lithuanians who were active in the Holocaust.

The Polish minority, although it is well accommodated in Lithuania in terms of Polish education and institutional settings for Polish culture, is still pursued by the shadow of pointless debates, often initiated by well-known linguists and historians from the Lithuanian establishment, about whether they are 'authentic' Poles or merely polonized Belorussians and Lithuanians. However, the historically-unprecedented improvement in the relations between the nation states of Poland and Lithuania was a result of a realistic foreign policy for the region pursued on both sides. This gives hope that the destructive ethnic debates will sooner or later be exhausted at least as far as the Poles are concerned.

In spite of the quest for adjustment to new global realities and above all the pressure from the European Union - Lithuania wants to apply for membership - there can be no miraculous recapture of Lithuania's multi-cultural past. Political and legal frameworks for minorities cannot easily displace the cultural and even metaphysical need for the Other, nor should they be too rashly taken as a sign of mature political and cultural tolerance. There is still important ground to cover if the defensive nationalist culture is to be replaced by Lithuania being seen as one of the big family of modern democracies: this requires the recognition of the Other as a positive asset.

Radical reform of Lithuanian society which will allow the country to compete on the global market and meet EU political and economic standards requires a full acceptance of a non-discriminatory, multi-cultural society: one that has come to terms with its recent past. (Reform has come at an even more drastic pace and with less scope for democratic debate in Estonia.) There has been a rush to placate the big institutions of the outside world in a necessarily superficial manner. For instance, social movements for new consumer and housing standards can have little meaningful impact as long as residues of twentieth century nationalism and its horrors have not been replaced. The now-marginalised socialist party, with its antiquated organisation and outlook, seems to be incapable of responding to the demands of the new social movements. Its discourse is fundamentally incompatible with that of the new generation of progressive opinion-makers. One sign of the times may be the newly elected president of Lithuania, who has brought with him a cosmopolitan and humanist background of experience.

There are even some signs in Lithuania and east central Europe more widely that the idea of multi-culturalism, and the region's rich tradition of multi-cultural and cosmopolitan cities such as Vilnius, Lviv and Gdansk, remains a radical democratic potential. (This idea of multi-culturalism is distinct from the specifically North American concept.) There is a hopeful belief that the rediscovery of the culture of cosmopolitan cities is just around the corner. This frame of mind is not least present in a new generation of young writers in the Ukraine and Poland. Yurii Andrukhovych's and Krzysztof Czyzhewski's respective essays on Lviv and Gdansk reveal multi-layered urban cultures, as well as multi-dimensionality. (Czyzhewski acknowledges that his realisation of multi-dimensionality, in the case of Gdansk, was influenced by his close reading of Gunter Grass's novels.) Most striking perhaps is that this new generation of writers are no longer inclined to view the nation-state as the only political frame for cultures in dialogue. These signs may pave the way for a new radical conceptualisation of democracy in East Central Europe. However, nobody should be deluded into believing that a democratic return is imminent. For the moment, the concept of the left will remain a relic of the recent past, and liberal cosmopolitanism will seem the road to radical utopia.

Social exclusion and multiple identities

Peter Weinreich

The commendable plans of the EU to achieve social inclusion through methods such as 'welfare to work' may, unintentionally, run into severe pitfalls. It is imperative that the political and cultural dimensions of these issues are brought to the fore. Peter Weinreich examines these dangers, and clarifies the possible ways of achieving the prerequisites of multiculturalism.

A facile multicultural or pluralist perspective permeates much thinking about communities in the nations of contemporary Europe. Contemporary welfare policies on education, the health service and welfare benefits assume a multicultural scenario of non-discrimination against ethnic and cultural minorities as an ideal. Current political thinking does not contend much with the implications of multiculturalism. It pays lip service to the social reality of diverse worldviews, alternative religions and divergent systems of moral values. At best, it holds to a superficial tolerance towards differing peoples.

The EU emphasis on social inclusion is an aspiration towards including people from any ethnicity within the social fabric of society. Inclusion without discrimination is the intention. However, the favoured interpretation of social exclusion narrows to that of *exclusion from the labour market*. The slogan *welfare to work* has much contemporary appeal.

This is solely an economic perspective concentrating on being excluded from work, or being unemployed. Social inclusion means people working. It is being economically independent. It is not remaining dependent on welfare benefits. This perspective implicitly assumes that inclusion in the labour market will also deal with issues of social exclusion. It appeals to legislation to combat wider discrimination based on race or gender. Economic inclusion in a non-discriminatory fashion would be the basis for social inclusion.

The paradox, and the danger, is that multiculturalism is reduced to a homogeneous ethos of an economic standard of labour market inclusion. This viewpoint considers the tensions of constitutional issues involving the coexistence of different ethnic identities within a community to be of secondary importance. EU directives are manifestly towards notions of economic inclusion, or including people within the labour market. The economic notion of the inclusive labour market relegates any other divisive tendencies to the imperfect functioning of democratic institutions.

The oral tradition in Europe

Bureaucratic blueprints for democratic institutions, although important in setting aspirations, will fail when they ignore the psychological realities of individuals in communities experiencing the day-to-day trappings of work or non-work, leisure, joys and tribulations of relationships, traumatic biographical events, and survival of an acceptable sense of one's identity. When these psychological realities coalesce around histories of common ethnic experiences, processes of social exclusivity will tend to outrank other factors of social exclusion such as unemployment.

Two inter-related factors leading to social divisiveness combine with an emotional intensity that requires psychological analysis, ethnic identity and primordialism. An understanding of the strength of passion involved in this combination is being developed within the Identity Structure Analysis (ISA) conceptual framework, which attempts to define psychological concepts that interface with societal and cultural phenomena.[1]

In ISA, one's ethnic identity is defined as that part of the totality of one's self-construal made up of those dimensions that express the continuity between one's construal of past ancestry and future aspirations in relation to ethnicity.[2] Ethnic identity is not fixed once and for all, but becomes modified and redefined down the generations according to current interpretations of the shared historical experiences of past ancestry and evolving cultural traditions. Cultural traditions are continually being updated from one generation to the next in the light of contemporary societal developments and future aspirations for the ethnic group in question. This is no bland viewpoint. If the person is a Jew, current interpretations of shared historical experiences include the Nazi holocaust; if Afro-Caribbean, then slavery and plantation; if Protestant British in Ulster, then the Battle of the Boyne. These historical events have not been experienced first-hand by contemporary generations, but they are recounted and handed down by grandparents and before them by their grandparents, which makes these events as vivid as ever through the oral history.

In the definition of ethnic identity, emphasis is placed on this being only a part of the totality of one's identity, which includes one's gender identity, occupational identity, familial identity and whatever other aspects of identity may be relevant. However, the strand of identity that is one's ethnic identity has an intergenerational continuity that other strands, such as gender and occupational identity, do not have. When intergenerational aspects of ethnic identity combine with sentiments of the primordialism of that identity, the psychological salience of ethnicity dominates the perception of human affairs.

Not all people are dominated by primordialism, which is not an explanatory notion but a sentiment that itself requires explanation. To clarify this, primordialism is defined as a sentiment, or affect laden set of beliefs and discourses, about a perceived essential continuity from group ancestry to progeny (perceived kith and kin), located symbolically in a specific territory

---

1. P. Weinreich, 'Rationality and irrationality in racial and ethnic relations: a metatheoretical framework', *Ethnic and Racial Studies*, 8, 1985, pp500-515; P. Weinreich, 'The operationalisation of identity theory in racial and ethnic relations' in J. Rex and D. Mason (eds), *Theories of Race and Ethnic Relations*, Cambridge University Press, Cambridge 1986, pp299-320.
2. P. Weinreich, 'Identity development in migrant offspring: theory and practice' in L.H. Ekstrand (ed) *Ethnic Minorities and Immigrants in a Cross-Cultural Perspective*, pp230-239, Swets & Zeitlinger, Lisse, The Netherlands 1986.

or place (which may or may not be the current place of the people concerned).[3] The power of primordialism, as a sentiment being felt and expressed by many people in the community, may be explained as an outcome of the very early identifications children make with those who shape their early experiences, in most cases their kith and kin. From the perspective of young children, these

'To view social inclusion as a by-product of good economic management is a mistake'

others have longevity stretching back before their consciousness, existing on a day-to-day basis, and promising to continue indefinitely into the future. The sense of the primordialism of kith and kin, hence ancestry, is psychologically the norm for the child, and remains so for the biographical child within the adult.

Many people, reflecting on and experiencing the convoluted histories of nation states, migrant groups, and changing national boundaries, adopt situationalism as a preferred perspective towards ethnic identity. Situationalism is defined as a set of beliefs or discourses about the instrumental and socially constructed nature of the group, in which interpretations and reinterpretations of history provide rationales justifying the legitimacy of a peoplehood.[4] However, in developmental terms, the sentiment of primordialism has precedence over situationalism from childhood through to adulthood. Many people do not relinquish primordial perspectives; those who do tend nevertheless to retain elements of a residual primordial sentiment. Certain cultural and historical circumstances for an ethnic group may combine to strongly engage individuals' primordial sentiments in relation to their ethnic identity.

Defining identity

In tackling social exclusion in terms of the labour market, the complexities of multicultural contexts, with their differing histories, are often neglected. The emphasis is on developing an inclusive labour market defended by democratic institutions. Across the European Union the divisiveness of primordial sentiments that people have regarding their national identities receives little

---

3. P. Weinreich, V. Bacova, and N. Rougier, *Primordial and situational ethnic identity: Political identification in Northern Ireland and Slovakia.* Paper presented to the Fifth European Congress of Psychology, 6-11 July 1997.
4. *Ibid.*.

attention. Within nation states the presence of multi-ethnic communities in which primordial sentiments are likely to figure strongly can lead to social exclusion. The emphasis on participation in the labour market as the dynamic of wider social inclusion is a flawed political concept. The reluctance to acknowledge 'difference' means that not enough consideration is given to the causes of social exclusion, with possibly tragic consequences. To view social inclusion as a by-product of good economic management is to misread the powerful psychological processes that orchestrate certain social structures of exclusion. These involve individual biographies related to broader ethnic experiences that take place within often painful historical scenarios. They proceed within difficult contemporary transformations in local, national and world structures. Genuine multiculturalism is more than the recognition of cultural dress and pastimes, accompanied by a liberal live and let live attitude.

The different histories of migrations are essential features of people's ethnicity, or sense of peoplehood. They will vary but may include slavery, racial and ethnic exploitation, uprooted refugee populations, religious oppression, genocide, or even moral superiority. In reconstructed form, the histories are social representations that define people's ethnic identity.

Identity involves a sense of biographical continuity in which reflection on one's past experiences provides a backdrop to one's future aspirations. Ethnic identity incorporates the continuity between handed-down experiences of one's ancestral heritage and imperatives for one's progeny in the future. Interpretations of historical events affecting one's ethnic group, together with derivative moral imperatives affecting oneself and one's offspring, necessarily dominate one's ethnic identity. They provide the context for the cultural beliefs that people have about the manner in which they should live their lives. Similarly cultural values are more than pastimes. They are matters of life and death in one's spiritual survival. They are based in deeply emotional wellsprings of identifications with influential agents. These identifications provide the context for one's own survival as a moral being, located within the longer-range historical context and subject to the immediate historical era. Since ancestry and progeny provide the personalised context for each person's biographical experience, the particular morality of gender relations that governs procreation constitutes a fundamental feature of the wider moral expression of a culture. Ethnic conflict perversely highlights the centrality of gender moralities in people's sense of ethnic identity. In the early 1990s in Bosnia-Herzegovina rape was employed as a weapon of war. The impregnation of women desecrates the moral integrity of the excluded people. Women were used as progenitors of the other ethnic group.

The danger is that an economic welfare-to-work conception of social inclusion will most likely be inadequate if it takes no heed of ethnic, national and constitutional tensions within and across nations of the European Union. If policy-makers do not understand and therefore do not take into account processes of maintaining one's ethnic distinctiveness in analyses of social exclusion, the consequences could be appalling. Governing parties will be powerless to counter populist appeals aimed at specific ethnic groups. This has the potential to exploit social divisions and could result in the breakdown of democratic social order. Social exclusion on economic grounds will seem mild compared with the exclusion of migrant communities in order to substantiate territorial claims on ethnic grounds or a nationality.

There is no reason whatsoever to have confidence that European democratic institutions, in their existing forms, can handle often competing tensions of pluralist communities. The different histories of European nations that account for shifting state boundaries and particular patterns of migration provide unique contexts for the nature of relationships between ethnic groups. Institutional structures that respond effectively to these contexts may or may not have been established. There is little consensus across nations about best practice. Compare the constitutional status of *Gastarbeiter* in Germany with the citizenship rights of individuals of migrant ancestry in the UK, and the banning of religious emblems - such as headscarves for Muslim girls - that contravene institutional secularism in French schools with tolerance of religious dress in schools in the UK.

With free labour mobility across national boundaries in the European Union, an added dimension to the local pluralist mix will be the previously unmet qualities of further alien cultures. Those of a liberal perspective will welcome this as an enrichment of cultural diversity. To those who feel their identity threatened cultural integration may prove too much to take. What this means for the nation states of Europe will very much depend on the ability of policy-makers to recognise and tackle the factors behind social exclusion.

Lettre de France

Alain Caillé

*Alain Caillé, together with Jean-Pierre Le Goff,
wrote a now-famous tract on the December 1995
uprising of trade unionists. It was called 'Le
Tournant de Decembre' and Caillé's part bore the
title 'Vers un nouveau contrat social?' ('Towards a
new social contract?') He takes a step further in
this analysis of the situation almost nine months
into the socialist regime headed by Lionel Jospin.
Caillé does not see any bold steps on the part of
Jospin's government to alleviate the precarious
situation of large sections of French society. If a new
social contract is to come into being, he argues,
then the initiative for the whole process must of
necessity come from below, where the energy for
social justice resides.Caillé's analysis of France is
evidently quite translatable to the general
conditions of the EU area.*

From an electoral viewpoint the left seems to be triumphing in Europe. It is associated with power in thirteen out of fifteen nations. And parties claiming to be leftist are in business in three of the more important nations - Italy, Britain and France. But this success leaves a bitter taste for all those who still want to believe in the humanist ideals of the traditional left. To be sure the magic recipe has not yet been found. The negative fight against unemployment has assumed the attitude that there exists no other choice than between the misery of low wages and an administrative sclerosis. It is for this reason that it may be valuable to pay attention to an initiative taken in France by about fifty intellectuals and well-known associated militants (and writers who between them have published more than one hundred books on the question of unemployment and the crisis of the social state), exploring a kind of third political way, equally distant from the all-market and the all-state approaches, and looking to find a broad consensus in an increasingly abused and maltreated European public opinion. They have now assembled around a European Appeal for a Pluralist Citizenship and Economy (AECEP), which has been translated into English, German, Italian, Spanish and Portuguese.

Each analysis, like every political tendency, represents a wide variation of views but contributors agree on the same diagnosis and on the same series of remedies. The diagnosis is that the crisis concerning work in Europe is of such a force and dimension that neither ultra-liberal nor classic Keynesian measures suffice to provide a remedy. Neither can reabsorb a scale of redundancy that is about to destroy our entire social and cultural equilibrium. Hence the necessity to put into action three series of reforms simultaneously.

◆ A significant reduction of the legal and effective duration of time at work, combined with a politics of active redistribution among salaried employees.

◆ The encouragement of a massive development of many non-profit activities by associations, interacting with both the private and public economies to provide for the emergence of a true pluralist economy instead of a purely market economy.

◆ The ending of the stigmatisation of the poorest and excluded sections of society by introducing a minimum wage.

It is on this third point that discussions - and opposition - have been the liveliest. But significantly it is also around this point that agreement has been reached in this Statement, with a common concern to oppose the perspective of workfare (in other words of obligatory work) which, since it began in the United States, has been gaining ground everywhere. Does not the experience of the nineteenth century show French national workshops and British workhouses to have been as inhuman as they were inefficient? It would be hardly reasonable to expect better from their contemporary counterparts. But it is in this direction of workfare and the liquidation of social assistance that the Blair government is now explicitly oriented, and towards which the European Commission is implicitly moving.

However, if we wish to oppose the return of such a social policy of a past age there is unfortunately little hope to be found in Jospin's political team. The two measures which the new government has taken in this direction - the reduction of working time to 35 hours and the creation of 700,000 jobs for young people in the social utility side of the service sector - represents a setback before it has even been clearly defined, adopted, and implemented. These measures have so far only inspired a lot of scepticism. After badly-conducted negotiations with the 'social partners' (that is the employers' association or CNPF) on the reduction of working time, the employers were provoked to end the talks. They concluded them by issuing a hostile declaration, whilst on the other hand the government failed to gain significant popular support. The whole deal was presented as if the reduction of legal working time was simply a technical matter, a technocratic gadget that could be expected to lead to a mechanical resumption in the recruitment of labour. This is something that is quite improbable. At the same time it is plain that this initiative cannot make sense if it is not 'owned' by the grassroots movement, as a goal desired in the name of social and human progress. As to 'employment for the young', the numbers involved in reality are substantially less than the figures announced. They essentially reduce themselves to what the government at all costs wanted to avoid - the disguised creation of new semi-public jobs with an unclear and undetermined status. That is, disguised and provisional administrative jobs at a discount price.

In writing into its programme the reduction of working time and the development of third sector social utilities, the Socialist Party, which up to the time of the elections had only shown hostility to these ideas, suddenly seemed to pay homage to the virtues of the 'pluralist economy' that was defended by AECEP. But in fact since the logic of it was not well understood, the Socialist government limited itself to adopting certain slogans while translating the principles into the only language it really understood. That is, the language of administrative economics. While determined to look into the future it nevertheless did not know how to get rid of the old reading-glasses. It also found itself deprived of arguments by the lack of enthusiasm which was expressed by the movement of the unemployed. This movement expects nothing out of the reduction of working time nor from the youth employment scheme (nor from the scheme for those over 25). It demands immediate responses to the increasingly intolerable misery, and to the absence of any perspective for dealing with it.

Certainly those movements which surfaced during the Christmas celebrations and which have brought power to the deprived had a ring of something familiar. It was as if their organisation had been managed by experts - gauchists, Trotskyites and militants from the CGT and the PCF, all of a sudden reassembled to play their part in some magisterial way. But the support of wider French society given to the movement of the unemployed - opinion polls show more than 70 per cent in favour of it - has nothing to do with political manipulation, and everything to do with a certainty that French society cannot much longer tolerate the general dissolution of the wage earner statute, and the rise of exclusion and racism, as well as the manifest powerlessness of the economic policies of both the political right and left.

The persistent question raised by the movement of the unemployed is exactly the one that the Jospin government thought could lead to a breakthrough. This is the question of the social minimum statute and more specifically the minimum wage (which in France exists under the name of RMI, Revenu minimum d'insertion). In the short term it is probable that the government, in which Communist ministers participate, will keep its unity by agreeing to a limited enhancement of social assistance. The recent rise in this has mostly made up for its decline in recent years, in fact with a margin to spare. But the failure to provide an increase in aid to support employment is just baffling, notwithstanding the inefficiency of various governments during the past 25 years. But the real problem is not so much a financial as a symbolic one. In what name and with what hopes should social assistance be distributed? On this account the CGT and the PCF are quickly facing the contradiction that has thus far prevented them from taking any active interest in the fate of the unemployed. The problem is how to demand definite rights to a significant minimum wage for the unemployed without risk of making perennial a situation of non-work that cannot make sense for the 'party of labourers'. Identical considerations explain the hostility on the part of the other trade union centres (FO and CFDT) to any organisational constitution that might provide representation for the unemployed.

Tony Blair's response to these issues appears to evoke only expressions of horror from the French Socialists (as from most people in Europe). But it does not appear as if the French Socialists have any other answer. Those Britons who are hostile to Tony Blair's moralising authoritarianism do not see much hope in that quarter. The French Socialists do not have the arms in their arsenal with which to fight the uphill struggle against the Blairite ideology. However those in the UK who want to oppose it should be aware that they are not alone. The important assembly of personalities who are operating in France (with authors such as André Gorz, Robert Castel, Dominique Méda, Serge Latouche, Jean-Marc Ferry, Jean-Pierre Dupuy, etc) for the platform of the Appeal (AECEP) are beginning to be met by a far-from-negligible echo from other parts of Europe - notably, from Italy (Marco Revelli, Gianni Vattimo, Pierpaolo Donati, Roberto Esposito etc), Germany (Claus Offe, Hans Joas, Rainer Zoll) and Spain. At this point it has become both desirable and necessary to discuss the drawing up of a constitution for a European movement capable of influencing this debate in time for the next European elections in 1999. We hope that substantial numbers of British participants will join.

Translated by Martin Peterson

Elusive solidarity in the French welfare state

John Crowley

In current debates about the future of the welfare state the French case is of particular interest, since its welfare state originated with a different approach from the other prototypical welfare nations. John Crowley analyses the distinctiveness and contradictions of the French situation

Reform of the welfare state has rarely been off the French political stage in the past twenty years. It has, indeed, been all over the place in both meanings of the phrase: multifaceted, complex, confused and confusing. The informed foreign observer is likely to be particularly puzzled by the curious disjuncture between the ideological framework within which the French tend to view their welfare system and the way in which it actually functions. Ostensibly, French welfare is governed by principles of solidarity and redistribution and a strong norm of equality. Indeed, a recent official report commissioned by the Balladur government identified the norm of equality as a major obstacle to reform, and suggested a reformulation of welfare principles on the basis of a supposedly competing principle of équité.[1] It sank without trace, and Jacques Chirac owed his election to the presidency in 1995 at least in part to the perception that his campaign commitment to reduce what he called the 'social fracture' meant reinstating the strong norm of equality. Nothing much actually happened, of course, but Chirac's defeat in the 1997 legislative elections showed that his promises had been taken seriously.

Y et the French welfare state is not strikingly egalitarian. It was only in 1990, for instance, that a guaranteed minimum income (the *Revenu Minimum d'Insertion*, or RMI) was created, following a wave of concern about extreme poverty and homelessness among those designated in media and official discourse as the 'nouveaux pauvres'. The UK, on the other hand, which the French regard as having weak or non-existent social protection, has had a system of universal income support, under various guises, since the inception of the welfare state. Similarly, in France, basic health insurance covers only around two-thirds of the cost of most forms of treatment (and sometimes much less): the rest must be paid for upfront, and reclaimed from private complementary insurance - which many people do not have - or the discretionary 'social fund', which like all discretionary mechanisms functions in a haphazard manner. Only now is a scheme for universal coverage (universal in the dual sense of 'all people' and 'full cost') being devised, but it is likely to be very narrowly targeted. Again the comparison with the UK is interesting. A final example, which will suffice for illustrative purposes, is the massive gap between rhetoric and reality with respect to issues of urban decay, to the point that an interpretation of the norm of equality as forbidding any form of targeted positive action may serve indirectly to legitimate certain forms of systematic inequality, or at least to shield them from serious academic and political analysis.

Rhetoric and reality

At the level of political discourse or intellectual-academic argument, it is very difficult to make sense of these apparent contradictions - although, as we shall see, the complexities of the French idea of citizenship are a major contributing

1. Commissariat général du Plan, *La France de l'an 2000. Rapport au Premier ministre de la commission présidée par Alain Minc*, La Documentation française / Odile Jacob, Paris 1994.

    The word équité is important. It was used by John Rawls' French translator to render 'fairness' (justice comme équité = justice as fairness), and the report explicitly refers to Rawls' 'difference principle', as a legitimation of certain kinds of inequality, to distinguish équité from égalité. The reading of Rawls is in fact singularly misinformed, but that has not made it any less influential.

factor. Indeed, in the self-styled country of Cartesian rationality and of the strong state, centralisation and uniformity, the situation is particularly puzzling. The most important reason is that the gap between rhetoric and reality is not empty, but filled by highly structured institutions and practices that are decisive in determining the mechanisms and implications of welfare. A closer look at the issues that have actually given rise to public debate in recent years is helpful in providing a fuller picture.

In fact, there are at least four distinct but interlocking debates, the peculiarities of which are often traceable to highly specific features of the historical development of the French welfare state.

(1) Debate about underlying principles is usually muted. The Minc report referred to earlier is an exception, as is the growing strength of an academic lobby for some form of citizen's income, justified by reference to considerations of social justice, of which André Gorz, Jean-Marc Ferry and Philippe van Parijs are representative figures.[2] Otherwise, principles are generally framed in terms of 'republicanism' - in other words the normative idea of *la République* reconstructed since the mid-1980s in the context of debates about immigration, globalisation and European integration.[3] Its characteristic features of equality and uniformity are interpreted by contrast with supposed Anglo-American 'liberalism' (by which the French mean free-market economics) and multiculturalism.

(2) A debate about structure is implicit in all recent discussions of welfare and occasionally comes out into the open. The organisation of the French welfare system as established after the Second World War is peculiar in that it does not reflect the centralised and nationalised ethos that led to the creation of monopolies such as *Électricité de France*, *Gaz de France*, or the *Société Nationale des Chemins de Fer*. Welfare is in theory decentralised both territorially and

---

2. *Misères du présent, richesse du possible*, Galilée, Paris 1997. *Qu'est-ce qu'une société juste?*, Seuil, Paris 1991.
3. For more detailed discussion, see John Crowley, 'Statehood and nationhood in contemporary France', in Louk Haagendoorn, George Csepeli & Henk Dekker (eds), *Nation, nationalism and citizenship in Western and Eastern Europe*, Utrecht, ERCOMER, 1998 (forthcoming).

functionally, and run at arm's length from the state. It is based on a series of autonomous bodies (responsible for pensions, health insurance, unemployment benefit etc), usually organised at the level of the *département*, which are formally run by committees representing employers' associations and trade unions on an equal basis (what the French call *gestion paritaire*). Representation of the various unions on the committees is determined by elections in which all employees - including foreigners - are entitled to participate, although a series of historical carve-ups also influences the division of responsibilities. From the point of view of the dominant Jacobin model of statehood, such a system is odd, and one would expect it to raise major issues of principle. In fact it is little discussed, and what discussion there is has tended to focus on the fairly trivial issue of whether some trade unions - *Force Ouvrière* being the prime suspect - use their representative positions for patronage.

Quite apart from this, such a fragmented system also gives rise to considerable practical difficulties in terms of funding. In order to maintain the fiction of autonomous management of the welfare system by the 'social partners' it is financed by a multitude of special levies or *cotisations* (for salaried employees there are currently some fifteen) each earmarked for a particular purpose (unemployment benefit, health insurance, pensions). The familiar problems of hypothecation result: each subsystem is either in surplus or in deficit, and some reallocative mechanism is required, which is necessarily an external imposition. Inevitably the state plays this role, since it defines the entitlements that the welfare system manages. Recent financing reforms have attempted to address this issue, but are restricted by the need to remain within the *paritaire* framework. The most important reform was the creation in 1989 of an entirely new levy - the Contribution Sociale Généralisée (CSG) - which is 'general' both in that it is levied on all incomes (whereas most other cotisations are levied only on wages) and in that it is not hypothecated to any particular purpose. This has gradually been extended and accounts for a steadily growing proportion of social-security revenue.

The third aspect of the structural debate is the absence of any clear framework for planning or controlling health expenditure, which is a direct consequence of the entrenchment of publicly funded private medicine: practitioners are paid by their patients, whom they attract (or fail to attract) on a purely market basis. All attempts to introduce some degree of control over expenditure have so far proved ineffective because of the huge power of the medical lobby and patients' preference for freedom of choice.

(3) The debate about funding is, in terms of political profile and of media column inches, the most significant, although, for the reasons just mentioned, the structure of the system leads to considerable confusion about what the problem actually is. Ostensibly, the issue is the social-security deficit, by which is meant the gap between expenditure and income raised by the various *cotisations* - a gap plugged by a combination of cost-cutting (which is unusual, and tends to involve the limiting of entitlements, rather than controlling expenditure directly - decisions in this case are taken at government level), higher *cotisations* (technically decided by the social partners), and transfers from general taxation, the latter of course making a nonsense of the supposed 'autonomy' of the system. There has been, more or less, one social-security plan a year since 1975, none of which has had any long-term impact. Recent debates about the deeper significance of funding have acquired greater prominence. To some extent, the overwhelmingly wage-based nature of the *cotisations* has been questioned: in a country where income tax accounts for only a very small proportion of overall tax revenues, such a funding system contributes to a tax system that is many respects regressive. The main reason for the CSG being, if not popular, then at least acceptable, is that it addresses this problem.

In addition, pensions have become a major concern. Since the entire French system, including the top-up schemes (*retraites complémentaires*) that are compulsory for all salaried employees, is based on redistribution, with annual income covering annual expenditure, the demographic timebomb is a very serious threat. However, funded pension schemes on the UK model - which have strong support from the insurance and financial-services lobbies - are ideologically suspect.

(4) Not always easy to disentangle from the first debate, but nonetheless distinct, is the recurrent question of the very principle of welfare, in the sense of the kind of society that France is, or could be, or should be - i.e. a debate about the very existence or relevance of solidarity, which is more general and abstract than a debate about the nature and content of solidarity, and tends to be framed in Eurocentric terms of 'civilisation'. One of the declarations made by Lionel Jospin after he unexpectedly became Prime Minister in June

1997 was that his purpose was to defend and revitalise a 'model of civilisation', defined by the contrast with a competing, and currently dynamic, model usually referred to in France as 'ultraliberal' - a term that encompasses even the mildest of free-marketeers. The UK, of course, is not judged to belong to the 'Europe' that would be threatened as a civilisation by the import of US, or for that matter Asian, values. Opposition to 'ultraliberalism' is indeed by no means limited to the left. Nothing approaching the radical conservative policies adopted by Reagan and Thatcher has affected France: monetarism and privatisation have indeed been embraced even by the left, but it is generally felt that these are technical issues that have no necessary social implications. Arguably the current crisis of the mainstream right, exemplified by its confused reactions to defeat in the 1997 legislative and 1998 regional elections, is a direct consequence. There is too little space between the pragmatic left and the xenophobic Front National for traditional French conservatism, and yet the 'Thatcherite' option, or something similar, is persistently ignored despite being the only viable medium-term strategy in strictly party-political terms.

It is not a gross exaggeration to suggest that France is stuck. Incremental reform - even if designed to ensure a *higher* degree of state control and a *higher* level of social protection - faces virtually insuperable institutional obstacles. Yet any serious clash with entrenched vested interests is often presented as the dismantling of the welfare state, a move which is both deeply unpopular and definitely off the political agenda, as the Juppé government found out to its cost in 1995.

How can France move forward from such a situation? The best starting point is to view the four themes discussed earlier as linked. Indeed it takes extraordinary obtuseness to discuss the issues separately, year after year, without their fairly obvious connections being pointed out. Such obtuseness is the immediate cause of the failure to implement changes that almost everyone agrees would be reasonable.

Where now for France?

At an empirical level, this fragmentation can be explained in terms of path dependency. There were sound pragmatic reasons, in the 1940s, to give employers' associations, trades unions, medical professionals and the insurance industry a vested interest in a fledlging welfare state that would probably have been depressingly easy to sabotage. However, once created, such a framework took on a life of its own and eventually became so entrenched that it could hardly be reformed at all. At a normative level, however, I think it has a deeper significance and supports a generalisable conclusion. It is natural to think of institutions - for instance those of the welfare state - as deriving from overarching norms by reference to which they can be shown to be pragmatically valid, or indeed to be ineffective and incoherent. This suggests a model of political conflict as being primarily about norms and the attempt to produce generally acceptable justifications for them, their subsequent implementation being a comparatively technical matter that does not recursively call the overarching norms into question. Such a model is consonant with the mainstream of contemporary political theory: it is explicit, in particular, in the work of John Rawls where it has a dual normative and analytical status, explaining both the social basis of conflict and appropriate ways of dealing with it. Whatever one may think normatively - certainly explicit debate about norms would seem far more 'rational' and potentially far more effective as an approach to reform of the French welfare state - the descriptive power of such a model is poor. The process in fact seems, in normal circumstances, to be precisely the other way around. I use the word 'normal' designedly here, since it points helpfully to a comparison with Kuhnian sociology of science. What is 'normal' about normal circumstances is that they involve a stable and largely unquestioned paradigm. Debate can be conducted without the parameters of debate themselves being brought into question, and contradictions and inadequacies can be swept under the carpet, or acknowledged merely as curiosities, without the stakes ever getting high. In other words, the institutions are effectively given and the process of making sense of them is not directly material to their continued existence. They have, almost literally, a life of their own.

What this means is that the institutions themselves have a kind of quasi-normative status. Thus, the inevitable contradictions between and within subsystems that are explained, but not justified, historically cannot be dealt with normatively in political debate. To put things rather differently, there is no basis on which policy debate can be made *zweckrational* or instrumental. An interesting sideline on this are French attitudes to Tony Blair (for French purposes synonymous with New Labour), who arouses huge curiosity - broadly positive on the right, broadly suspicious or hostile on the left. There is persistent misunderstanding of Blair as being some kind of pragmatist because of statements such as 'there is no such thing as left-wing or right-wing economic policy - just good policy and bad policy' (in his speech to the French National Assembly in March 1998). The explicit core of Blair's creed - that institutions and policies have purely instrumental status and that only values count politically - which if anything marks him as a highly ideological politician, passes almost unnoticed. It only makes sense in a post-Thatcherite context where all institutions can be seen as up for grabs, because all (or nearly all) have been fairly profoundly reformed in recent memory. Not having been through the shake-up, France is simply deaf to the message.

'France seems to be stuck - incremental reform faces virtually insuperable institutional obstacles'

To put this in more concrete terms: the French are strongly attached to the mechanisms of their welfare state. In the field of health, which is probably the most important, they regard such things as free choice of a GP (and freedom to see an unlimited number of GPs in one day if they so desire), unrestricted direct access to specialists, and the absence of waiting lists as being sacred, not because of any principles that they supposedly embody, but *per se,* because they are in themselves principles. They are entrenched institutional entitlements, as distinct from abstract individual rights. The fact that it is very difficult to make sense of them in terms of solidarity (although of course no one denies that freedom of choice is, other things being equal, a good thing), to the extent that the undoubted waste they contribute to makes it more difficult to underwrite universal health insurance, is met with a collective and very Gallic shrug, as a detailed analysis of media debate would show. The most revealing recent issue was the attempt by the Juppé government in 1995-96 to introduce a very modest degree of control over expenditure based on targets for practitioners, subject in principle to financial penalties, and limits to GP-shopping for patients. In order to police the latter a health booklet (*carnet de santé*) was issued to all adults. It was intended as a portable medical record and was designed to reduce wasteful duplication of such things as blood tests. It is in principle compulsory for the practitioner to record in each patient's *carnet* details of each visit. In fact, both practitioners and patients have boycotted the scheme (which any outside observer would regard as eminently sensible), and the state has in effect, albeit tacitly, scrapped it.

Conversely, this Kuhnian angle offers a helpful definition of what a 'crisis' would be. Institutions, it suggests, tend to break down or to lose their legitimacy when they conflict directly, and not merely by their practical implications, with norms that can be powerfully articulated in the political arena - which in practice also means with powerful political interests. Technical malfunctions, waste, inefficiency; none of these, if we follow the above reasoning, lead in themselves to institutional crisis. This is important if we follow the many writers over the past two centuries who have suggested that fundamental reform in France is necessarily the product of crisis. It took a near revolution in 1968 to produce institutional reform of higher education.

To the extent that the majority of French people are still beneficiaries of the system and that only a minority are on the wrong side of the 'social fracture', there is no obvious crisis of legitimation, and therefore no serious prospect of reform. Chirac's 1995 presidential campaign has been interpreted as disproving this analysis, but subsequent events - notably the collapse of the 1995 Juppé plan to reform social security, which extended far beyond the *carnet de santé* mentioned earlier - hardly support the thesis. Similarly the bottoming out of electoral support for the Communist Party and the growth of the far left vote have been seen as signs of a major shift in public opinion. One should remember though that the Front National share of the vote has progressed equally fast.

This kind of political fragmentation, resulting from institutions being so fundamentally interwoven with society, probably exists in all countries, because of the intimate, organic relation between the modern state and welfare, of which the idea of social citizenship - understood analytically rather than normatively - offers an articulation. British pride in the National Health Service, for instance, has similar features, and tends equally to focus on institutional aspects such as free treatment rather than explicitly normative issues. The biggest obstacle to the development of any kind of truly transnational framework for welfare - for instance at the European level - is indeed precisely this. France, however, also exhibits an unusual degree of *intellectual* fragmentation.

The main reason is the virtual absence of the paradigm of social citizenship that, drawing on various readings of T.H. Marshall, has become central in English-language political theory and philosophy. The idea that systems of rights might be self-legitimating on the basis of ideas about social membership, and that welfare in that sense might be constitutive of modern statehood rather than incidental to it (as, say, agricultural or industrial policy is), conflicts sharply with powerfully entrenched French conceptions of statehood and nationhood that are shared by most sections of the ideological spectrum. There is a tension between political and social citizenship that has been explored by theorists such as Jürgen Habermas and Claus Offe, and to which French debate, albeit in often cruder terms, is highly sensitive. In addition, Marshall's framework has been appropriated, somewhat dubiously in terms of his own work, by a postnational line of theory that regards social rights as a key component of a form of citizenship beyond the nation state.[4] In France, on the other hand, for reasons that are traceable to debates about immigration and integration in the context and in the wake of the 1987 Commission on Nationality, the nation state has been revived as a central - albeit not unchallenged - point of reference. As matter of fact, Marshall's classic scheme of tripartite division and historical progression applies quite well to the empirical development of citizenship in France, but his conceptual framework remains largely alien.

The best way of looking at this in concrete terms is to focus on current debates about social exclusion, which I shall illustrate primarily with reference to the particularly difficult problems raised for the principles and practices of the French welfare state by post-migratory processes in the context of urban decay - what the French summarise as the question of the *banlieues*.

Social citizenship

It is impossible to discuss here in detail the social problems themselves. As represented in mainstream political debate, however, they can be summarised quite easily. The central issue is perceived to be the crisis of social mobility (*promotion sociale*, as the French usually call it), leading to the hardening of boundaries between class fractions and thus the quasi-hereditary entrenchment of social difference. This emphasis can easily be misunderstood as indistinguishable from contemporary Anglo-American middle-classism. In fact,

---

4. John Crowley, 'The national dimension of citizenship in T. H. Marshall', *Citizenship Studies*, 2(2), 1998 (forthcoming).

social mobility has a strongly Republican connotation: its highest expression is not enrichment, but success in the education system, crowned by the *concours* that recruit the technocratic élite. Thus the state, rather than the market, is the primary locus of mobility. Even within the private sector, a similar bias is perceptible. At least in large companies, status tends to be more important in terms of differentiation than financial gain - and status is generally based primarily on educational attainment. The best illustration is the untranslatable term *cadre*, which while it originally applied to people on the basis of their position in the organisation (*encadrement* meaning effectively command structure) has now become purely status-oriented. Graduates, for instance, are hired as *cadres*, even though they usually have no management responsibilities; and conversely departments may be run by people who, having risen up the ranks without having been to university, are not regarded as *cadres* despite performing the function of *encadrement*.

When envisaged in this way, the crisis of social mobility has profound ideological significance. If some idea of equality is central to mainstream French conceptions of statehood and nationhood, and if the French state is in fact hierarchical and, with respect to civil society, authoritarian, legitimation becomes a key problem, and one not easily solved. Social mobility, if generally believed in, does the trick, since it normatively produces hierarchies of competence based on the authority of intelligence. However mythological the belief may be - a large body of work by Pierre Bourdieu and his associates has shown the extent to which élite reproduction nestles snugly in the formal principle of mobility - it has long functioned very effectively. Conversely, if it is now beginning to erode, the stakes are very high. Statehood and nationhood, and not simply, say, the education system or administrative structures, are in question.

These perceptions also provide the framework for the dominant French discourse about immigration and its consequences, which often puzzles foreign observers. The children of immigrants, because of the historical, social, economic and geographical circumstances of their parents' migration, tend to live in the *banlieues*. Thus marginalised they are at the sharp end of the crises within the core mechanisms that have historically underwritten a degree of status mobility sufficient to legitimate the French state: the education system and the labour market. And for them, unlike for those in similar circumstances who can take refuge in culturalist or racist nationalism, no other mechanism is available. Indeed, they are the targets of the compensating mechanisms from which they are specifically excluded. Hence the view that the very existence of what the French often call the 'second generation' is symptomatic of a broader crisis of nationhood. In the ideal nation, ethnicity - whether 'French', as exemplified by Front National discourse, or 'minority' - would cease to exist. Hence, also, the central position given to 'the school' (*l'école*, which refers inseparably to both the institutions and the processes of education) in political debates about immigration: thus, notoriously, the exorbitant significance attached to the 'headscarves' affair of the early 1990s.

It is a direct consequence of this set of perceptions that welfare is generally regarded as peripheral to issues of social exclusion or integration. Policy in these areas has consistently focused on the reform of the labour market and the education system, and on background measures designed to reduce geographical disparities in access to jobs and education (tax incentives for business start-ups, housing renovation, infrastructure improvements, etc). It has on the whole been timid and largely ineffective, but the ideological and institutional parameters leave little scope for radical innovation. The suspicion that welfare entrenches and legitimates inequalities is very powerful in France, even though the reasons may be quite different from those familiar from US and UK debate. Thus, controversy about 'RMI dependency' started almost as soon as the minimum-income scheme had been introduced. Furthermore, any form of targeting that could be interpreted as entrenching social difference, in other words, as recognising the huge gap between the real world and the ideal of equality, is equally suspect. The unease about discussing discrimination against French citizens of foreign origin - which contrasts oddly with massive academic and political interest in the ideological aspects of racism - is the starkest illustration of this. The technicalities of the welfare state express and reinforce its ideology. The whole ethos of the system is contributory and insurance-oriented rather than redistributive in any strict sense, and this makes *solidarité* in the French sense the opposite, rather than a version, of social citizenship. It is about collective risk-management, not equality; and conversely equality is conceived in terms of civil and political status and not social outcomes.

Welfare is peripheral to French conceptions of statehood and nationhood, which offer no coherent basis for welfare reform, and which cannot accommodate without major revision any strong idea of social citizenship. The likelihood of such revision appears small - despite the broadly favourable context of European integration - in view of the huge intellectual investment since the late 1980s in the reinvention or reformulation of the French *républicain* ideal. Citizenship as a stato-national status conceived primarily in political terms has very deep ideological and sociological roots. In many ways, current debates about welfare reflect a recurrent search for some embodiment of the forgotten third term of the revolutionary slogan '*Liberté, Égalité, Fraternité*'. Yet solidarity as brotherhood raises difficulties. In a provocative but persuasive series of books, the social anthropologist Emmanuel Todd has attempted to explain the ideologies and politics of contemporary France in terms of deeply rooted family structures. He suggests that the social matrix of the idea of the *République* is the nuclear-egalitarian family of the pre-revolutionary Northern French peasantry. This was characterised by liberty (of adult children from parental control) and equality (between siblings). *Fraternité*, and therefore solidarity, is thus elusive because it is ultimately empty: it is simply the sum of *liberté* and *égalité*. This proves nothing, of course, but, as the French say, *ça fait réfléchir*.

Waiting for Mandela

Social exclusion and resistance in the 'new' Sweden

Ove Sernhede

Sweden's once cohesive and egalitarian society is not coping with recent economic shocks, and its citizens of non-Swedish origin are suffering the consequences.

For many postwar decades Sweden was a model of egalitarian economic policies, and Swedes were well-known for their social conscience and humanitarian approaches to the weak, the socially excluded. Among the latter Swedish social policy counted political refugees and other immigrants. Today there is intense debate about whether it was a fundamental wrong committed against immigrants to treat them as inherently weak upon arrival in Sweden. It is clear, a priori, that in order to make the choice of going a long way abroad to a strange nation in an inhospitable climate it takes quite a bit of both competence and strength. This evidently means that the social policy approach must have been flawed from the start. Immigrants should have had both a fair chance and a platform to create new institutions and enterprises. There is evidence for such an argument in the fact that before 1990, when Sweden was plunged into the deep mire of a largely self-inflicted structural economic crisis, the immigrant population had a larger proportion in employment than Swedes. The 1990s crisis caused, overnight, ills not known until then in postwar Sweden, including extremely high unemployment, *of which the immigrant population was accorded a disproportionate share. With the parallel rise of ghettoisation and a new pathological racism, the large population of second generation immigrants[1] began to see themselves as the real victims and as the new underclass in a now prototypical crisis nation. Swedish officials and politicians were too inexperienced to handle the situation properly. They created the involuntary impression of encouraging an opportunist racism in the state apparatus. Swedish civil society, by and large, has reacted strongly against the sometimes gross faux pas committed against immigrants by the state. The second-generation immigrants, who see their chances in Swedish society being reduced to zero, have reacted strongly. Ove Sernhede, a leading Swedish scholar in cultural studies, presently does research in suburbs where immigrant density is very high. His findings have a disturbing bearing upon the state of present social democratic societies. They also clearly demonstrate the necessity of multicultural societies, with multi-cultural constitutions.*

Sweden does not need any apartheid laws, there are no laws needed forcing immigrants to live in certain locations. It is already a fact that all the black-heads are living separately, so the effect is just the same as the one that existed in South Africa. So, listen man - Hammarkullen or Hjallbo are like the Soweto of Gothenburg ... with one difference - we have no Mandela.

Muhammed, 20 years of age, from Somalia

New patterns of poverty in Europe

Since the middle of the 1980s there has raged an intense debate among sociologists and other social scientists about patterns of marginalisation and poverty on the European continent as well as in the United Kingdom. The development towards post-industrial society has implied a growing social polarisation in many countries. The rise of new forms of social exclusion has pushed an increasing number of groups into marginalisation and ultimately into exclusion. The forms and intensities involved in this process of mounting class differentiation do vary; but it is possible to discern certain common

---

1. For a discussion of the Swedish term *'invandare'* (translated as immigrant in this article), see note 1, p98.

tendencies in the emerging new Europe.

In order to explain this development, politicians regularly and compulsively refer to the 'economic crisis'. But, at the same time, Gross Domestic Product has witnessed strong growth in the entire European Union during the past few decades. Luxury and poverty have always existed side by side. However, the present situation offers something new, in the growing gaps between the world where people live in affluence and the one where scarcity prevails. Neither millionaires nor the destitute have at any time during the postwar period been so many as now. According to official statistics there are 52 million poor people, 17 million unemployed and 3 million homeless in the EU. These figures are rising every day - at the same time as an improved competitive position has put the economy of the EU into a strongly expanding phase.

A background element of importance in this development is the new international division of labour. In addition, the new IT sector is putting greater demands on labour. Economies require highly qualified people with an exponentially rising competence while a number of tasks in traditional industries are eliminated. The consequence is that there are no jobs for a rising army of redundant citizens. The effect on immigrants and refugees who in recent years have moved to the suburbs of European cities is that they too are facing growing difficulties in entering the labour market. The permanency of contemporary patterns of poverty is clearly linked to globalisation. This 'modernised misery' has emerged independently of what the economies happen to look like. Those who have carried the new destitution on their shoulders have easily been disarmed by their marginal positions and their heterogeneity, which have facilitated their exclusion from societal processes by the established actors of the political system. The political machines of established interests find it menacing to be in any sense identified with or still less a mouthpiece of the 'modern misery'.

Immigration, alienation

The dismantling of the institutions of the welfare state is at the root of contemporary poverty. What Scott Lash has called an institutional deficit is particularly evident in urban, ghetto-like environments where 'modern misery' is more manifest. The American scholar William Julius Wilson has stressed the pattern of synchronisation between developments in Europe and the United States. On the other hand his French colleague Joic Wacquant has found decisive differences. One important such difference is constituted by the heterogeneous nature of ghettos in Europe. Thus the demarcation lines between those socially excluded and the rest of society do not clearly coincide with the categories of race or ethnicity as in the US. A theoretical debate to define what constitutes a class or a ghetto is not crucial in establishing the emergence of a new underclass, and the ghettoisation of Europe. Lash is asking where and when, rather than if, the European version of Rodney King will occur - in Berlin, Marseilles or Rotterdam?

Those marginalised groups of mobile immigrants or refugees who are labelled the 'new underclass' in Britain, or the 'new poor' or the 'outcasts' on the Continent, have during the past ten-year period been forming ghettos everywhere in Europe - Moss Side (Manchester), Niewe Westen (Rotterdam), Bobigny (Paris) and Gutleutviertel (Hamburg), Rinkeby (Stockholm), Angered (Gothenburg) and Rosengard (Malmo). All these mentioned territories are involved in a territorial stigmatisation process. Discourses in the media, and society more widely, are demonising the conditions of life in these areas in a way that is creating fright and insecurity both inside and outside them. Moral panics are created by stereotypes about criminality, race, culture and religious antagonisms, which exacerbate conditions still more for people already sidetracked by poverty and alienation.

The situation in metropolitan areas in Sweden - Stockholm, Gothenburg and Malmo - is that 40 per cent of all children and young people under 17 years of age live in 'exposed urban districts', in the words of a parliamentary committee on 'big city conditions'. The majority of people in these districts have overseas backgrounds. The largest share of youngsters with immigrant origin is to be found in districts with extremely low incomes. The disposable income among families with children in Rosengard (Malmo) was 156,000 Swedish kroner (£15,000) lower in 1994 per annum than the average income in the city of Stockholm. In Gothenburg and Malmo, there are districts with extremely low incomes, where more than 50 per cent of children between 0-6 years of age have unemployed parents, and these are areas with a 90 per cent immigrant population. These circumstances have put Sweden into a state of shock. The so-called Swedish model is dead. The situation can of course not be compared to conditions in the United States, where the life of every second black child is one of deprivation. Nevertheless the idea of the Swedish 'peoples' home' is being crushed. Sweden has for some time also been entering the two-thirds society. The full employment of 1990 became, in real terms, 12-15 per cent unemployment overnight. In Gothenburg, a classic working-class city with half a million inhabitants, of whom 100,000 are immigrants, social entitlements increased by 100 per cent between 1990 and 1993.

'A territorial mythology is cultivated, a kind of "nationalism of the neighborhood"'

Research on the new poverty areas in the European metropolitan districts suggests that, in contrast with the traditional working-class quarters, where poverty was an integrated part of the culture, the new ones are suffering from a lack of solidarity and community spirit. The local, collective and territorial identity, which earlier provided security and a feeling of self-assertiveness, is now replaced by instability in the very same districts. There is an uncertainty, and alienation in relation to the rest of society; and, within the neighbourhoods, conditions are affected by competition and conflictual antagonisms between different groups. These patterns can certainly be discerned in Sweden. The new high-immigrant-density suburban districts in the three metropolitan areas constitute fragile communities characterised by extreme ethnic heterogeneity. Many people see their living in a particular district as a temporary solution, and thus the social space of the district represents a rather weak basis for any community spirit. Instead, it is the family and the commonalty of the ethnic group to which they belong that is charged with a new meaning.

The Hammer Hill Click

Things are different for the young. In the nursery, everyone plays with everyone else, and in school you cooperate with students from a different ethnic background. During leisure time you are out in the streets and cultivate companionships which supersede the ethnic boundaries drawn by parental culture. All young people are at a stage in their lives when they are seeking both their outer and inner selves. In these multi-ethnic areas the constant encounters with young people from other cultures, with Swedish society, and with what is now a global and media-saturated youth-culture, imply that new points of departure are created for the identification processes which are embedded in the adolescent work of identity.

One of the more salient features among the contact groups I have observed during the year I studied immigrant youth in Hammarkullen, Angered (the major ethnically mixed suburb), is their reflexivity and openness. They readily absorb and test out the different expressions, articulations and views of the world inherent in different cultures. In the area where I have spent most time, a group of 12 boys between the ages of 17 and 20 has created a hip-hop collective, which for preference makes rap-music. The members of the group have their backgrounds in Africa, Latin America and the Middle East. They regard themselves as constituting an ethnic alliance, the task of which is not only to represent the young from Hammer Hill (as which they have literally rebaptised their district) but to speak for all immigrant youth from all suburbs in the whole of Sweden. This collective aptly calls itself 'The Hammer Hill Click' (sic) and it is working very hard to create respect and goodwill for the suburb to which they belong. Their loyalty to the area (district) won't be budged. A territorial mythology is cultivated that constitutes a kind of 'nationalism of the

Kollektiv-Hammer Hill by Cicci Jonson

neighbourhood', which is strongly reminiscent of the way working-class lads used to launch their strategies to symbolically charge the quarters in which they were brought up.

To be a 'click' implies that they, in spite of their different origins and creeds, are an inseparable unit. Within this Click, everyone has a fundamental right to claim his or her religious or ethnic particularity and to represent any branch of rap-music as long they are loyal to the defined common task of the group. This assignment is to regard oneself as a soldier with the music as a weapon, or to be as the Click says 'microphone prophets'. The texts of the group deal with police brutality, discrimination and racism in Swedish society; and they embrace friendship and gang solidarity, reverence to Allah and Islam, the history of Latin America, everyday life in the suburb and so on. The group are issuing a mini-CD and one of the songs is entitled '88-soldiers'. When I ask what they mean by that title one of the Latin Americans of the group responds, 'Man, you must think, think for yourself, what do you think Man?'

After some intense thought, which leads me to dismiss the explanation that they are identified with their other comrades as the 88 persons, I realise that the meaning has to do with the symbolism in figures which the neo-nazis employ when they render cryptic greetings to Hitler. H is the eighth letter in the alphabet and 88 is consequently HH or Heil Hitler. Thus I ask if that is not just something that the nazis use to praise Hitler? The whole gang bursts out into laughter and one of them says:

Man, you are a wimp, sure - we rip those symbols off the nazis and create total confusion for them, you dig Man. In one year's time, they cannot any longer go around in the city with their 88-tattoos for we have snatched their symbols. For us 88 means Hammer Hill and 88-soldiers represents our being soldiers, the soldiers of Hammarkullen and we are ready for war. We have had enough, we don't want to take all this crap any more, do you get it Man, you get it. In this song everybody is there, all 12 have their own rhymes about their own thing. Muhammed and B-boy speak for the blacks, for their people and their religion ... you hear that they rap around Allah and 'breaking the law' and ... then we latinos are coming with the message to our people about the brown ones, you understand Man ... then we are creating certain rhymes together so it becomes 'niggaz and latinos got to unite n'fight' and that sort of thing, you get it Man. You know, the song begins with different sounds like that, then it eases its way over to violins, beautiful and disturbing like that, then there are sounds showing that there is a war going on, you understand, and then we come in and talk coolly, first stating that we are not going to take any more crap and then ... we get really going...

The title of the other song is 'El Mesage' (The Message) and is written by two of the latinos of the group. The lyrics tell about the fate of the native South Americans, that is the same as that of the blacks from Africa. Their history is a parallel one: of plundering and enslavement by white people, by Europe. Even if these latino young people are not of native South American origin, the identification with native South Americans remains total. The song starts with an aggressive Spanish guitar, which symbolises the scent of gold and the hubris of the conquistadores. Gradually this accord gives way to a native South American melody-line which becomes stronger and clearer. This folklore inspired melody is played on an old native South American string instrument and symbolises resistance on the part of the original peoples of South America. The song is in praise of those native peoples of South America who were driven back further and further into the Andes and whom the Spaniards never managed to subdue. The rhythmic base is a heavy, modern rap. Two more songs are included on the CD: 'One is more commercial you know, like more funky gangsta-shit, and it is named "West Coast Slang", whereas the name of the other is "Pig hunting season" and it deals with police hostility towards us and how we are against the police.'

The most palpable feature of my contact with this multi-ethnic hip-hop collective remains their definition of themselves as representatives and spokesmen of a new, ethnic underclass. In one sense, they are unusual. There are few other politically articulate young immigrant groups who see themselves as 'soldiers', and they create a multi-ethnic cultural expression as an armoury of weapons. In another sense, they are a quite a common phenomenon. In several corresponding living quarters around Sweden similar meetings and fusions take place. Each area has its specific conditions, its specific history and its particular ethnic composition. It is this aspect which makes the cultures which the young are creating in their encounters seem different in different areas. But although the local variation is great, there are still certain fundamental patterns in most of the high-density immigrant suburbs, irrespective of their location in Stockholm, Gothenberg or Malmo. One feature is the subordinated role of girls in these street cultures. Another striking feature is the identification with, and the impact of, life styles and ideals which have taken shape in the frustrations, and wrath of North American ghetto culture.

Black culture, white youth

From cultural research we know that youth subcultures, both in the United States and in Europe, have, since the interwar period, been inspired by, and have even taken over, elements of Afro-American culture. From the emergence of the first modern youth cultures in the USA of the 1920s - when the black hot-jazz was the centre of interest - through to bebop, rhythm-and-blues, soul, funk, and reggae, and up to the rap music of today, Afro-American music has constituted a central element in nearly all white youth cultures. Hip-hop, or the culture within which rap-music has grown, today appears as the increasingly obvious underclass culture of global urbanity. This is also true in Sweden. Today young men not only listen to 'black music', they also walk, speak and dress like Afro-Americans, more than ever before. Some have acquired the label 'white niggers' or 'wiggers' whereas others call themselves 'black albinos'. For instance by claiming that 'blackness is a state of mind', and not of the skin, the more reflexive and articulate parts of this youth-culture deconstruct given perceptions and reach, through proclamatory statements, song texts and the like, into that academic discussion which has long since maintained that race and ethnicity are political and cultural constructions.

During previous decades the middle class often dominated amongst jazz freaks and blues or soul fanatics. They found in black culture an exotic flavour, which came in handy as a means to defy and challenge the parental culture. The remnants of this pattern still exist of course, but what is new is that it is no longer the young of the middle class who dominate the interest in Afro-American culture. This is rather the mission of the new immigrant youth, who certainly also cultivate romantic ideas of ghetto culture. However, the decisive element for the identification of these youngsters with this particular culture is not exoticism. Instead, it builds on a real analogy between one's own situation and the one of the black population in the USA. Their fascination with the Afro-American culture is founded on its aesthetic expressions, which work as a point of departure for the formulation of their own experiences of alienation and discrimination; its cultural codes are immersed in resistance, and offer alternatives to the established identity and life patterns of Swedish society.

For many of these young people, traditional institutions, parties and ideologies do not appear credible, or as in any way created for them. 'You know I actually know a lot about politics but I may never be recognised for that. You only have to look at the Swedish parliament to see how many blackheads you'll find there ... the normal and ordinary sort of politics is not for us' - this was Santos, a Latin American 20 year old. Santos speaks with some authority since he has lived in Sweden since the age of three. For him, as for many of his friends, ghetto culture (black as well as hispanic) appears as the only adequate expression for political resistance. Those poses, jargons and attitudes offer, albeit in a menacing way, a counter-identity that invokes respect.

'Some call themselves "white niggers" or "wiggers", others call themselves "black albinos"'

The identification with Afro-American culture does, however, contain a dualism. On the one hand, it appears as if the openness of this culture, its 'call-and-response' structure, conveys embryos of new cultural models and symbolic communities. Its aesthetic codes, in particular evident in the music, constitute a language that, in certain respects, loosens up ethnic boundaries, or builds bridges across them. Such processes may create new forms of alliances and amalgamations. Herein we find a potential that may function as a basis for constructive dialogues and learning processes between the youngsters who employ these cultural patterns and Swedish society.

On the other hand, we can also see how marginalisation and powerlessness contribute to the creation of a fascination with the criminal gang culture of the ghettos, which can act to reinforce alienation, exclusion and segregation. The tendencies towards hostility to the dominant culture, which already exist in some circles where many immigrant youngsters grow up, can be reinforced through an identification with the most unrelenting and violence-centred aspects of ghetto culture. It may thus cement, and give legitimacy to, already existing hostile and confrontational stances. This is all the more likely if the growing tendencies of segregation and marginalisation cannot be halted.

Increasing numbers of young people of immigrant origin will face growing difficulties in entering Swedish society. Many already find themselves in an impasse, and see no other way but to turn against society. Few have the constructive and articulate political ambition of The Hammer Hill Click, who, via their rap-music, are knocking on the door to be let into Swedish society.

Street masculinity

One aspect of identifications with LA gangland culture is the shaping of heterosexuality and masculinity by gangster rap. To become a man is today a much more open process than ever before. The traditional patterns of male identity have been brought into question. This has added to the complexity of the situation immigrant boys are faced with. These youngsters are forced to develop identities of their own amongst a barrage of premodern and postmodern male images. Modern insecurity can often produce an exaggerated masculinity. In gangster rap, this overcompensating form of maleness is expressed in insatiable sexual appetite and a brutality which seeks to terrorise the established order. This glued-on masculinity represents a defence against a deeper insecurity in relation to one's own sex, which is handled by a 'blowing-up' of an omnipotent image. This is typical of family patterns where the father role model is weak or totally absent and where the mother, who takes the needs of the family as the main point of departure for her behaviour, takes a dominant role within the family.

Even though we know that research on rap has not made much progress towards conveying truths about reality in the multi-ethnic suburbs of Sweden, there is enough evidence to claim that similar patterns occur in Sweden as in the United States.

The rap text 'Havin' no love, my home became the family I never had' states that in order to survive the big city ghetto jungle you have to belong to a gang. When the father is gone, it is in the clan or the gang that safety is created and the male identity is confirmed. These fatherless fraternity clans constitute the only valid authority for their members. The central aspects of masculinity are fostered through the gang, which also provides strict choreographic and ritualised patterns of behaviour for the grounding of male identity. The group also offers protection, or a free-zone, where a failing identity may be recharged and respectless fantasies enacted which involve aggressions against all representations of the segregating majority and freedom-curbing authorities. The gang is also at the heart of the street mythology and bad-boy image that the gangster-rap has developed and launched with great commercial success.

One of the key myths in rap culture is the rapper as homeless 'on the edge living street kid', the miserable child of society whom only rap-music can save and bring to a new life - it may even enable him to become the spokesperson of his people and culture. Practically all great rap-artists have this background, which provides them with the insights to illustrate life conditions in the ghetto. When this is combined with their intellectual craft, and their street-wiseness, they are able to analyse society at large. Marshall Berman even suggests that one of the reasons for the embrace of rap-music by non-blacks is that rap is one of the few voices in the USA today which tells the 'truth' about social evils in American society. The contemporary Swedish suburban rapper identifies himself with the same task and mission.

Concluding remarks

The currents of migration, processes of marginalisation and patterns of segregation which have profoundly transformed Sweden during the 1990s tend to make immigration almost synonymous with social exclusion. Comparing the Swedish situation with developments in France, the French sociologist Etienne Balibar denotes these conditions as 'racism without race'. The young immigrant men whom I interviewed in 'Los Angered' (a pun referring to the large high-density-immigrant suburb Angered in Gothenberg) are not expecting anything from - nor of - Swedish society. They are conscious, and strongly critical, of the enforced ethnic boundaries which are transforming social inequality into cultural differences. And the jargons and attitudes of ghetto culture are offering a counter-identity for those who have been consigned to the position of second class citizens through the operations of the two-thirds/one-third society

Cultures developed by the young are making visible antagonisms and conflicts which exist below the surface of society. In this sense, youth culture can be compared to a seismographic instrument. For young people in the suburbs of the metropolitan areas remain in many respects quite invisible in spite of their forming themselves into expressive cultures. Segregation has sent them off to delimited reservations where they have very restricted contacts with the surrounding society. Under such circumstances music and other cultural expressions become doubly important. Culture may provide an opportunity to express and influence one's situation and symbolically ease the pressure of frustration. However, culture is also a channel for communicating one's situation to others, and for making it known to the rest of society. One important aspect of working to break patterns of segregation is the creation of opportunities which offer young people a chance to portray and profile themselves, and to create new arenas where they can perform and become visible.

In this way communications can come about between these immigrant and other Swedish young people. This is of crucial importance since the appearance and growth of this new youth culture represents a severe criticism of the development of society during the past decade, and one to which we can no longer turn a blind eye. There exists a tendency in public political discourse to deny the adverse developments of the past few decades. This denial is founded on the desire to view this phenomenon as only representing a slight deviation. Soon the old order, it is claimed, will be restored. Such an unrealistic approach is common. It is high time to erase people's illusions, but it is too late to debate whether this development is good or bad - this simply *is* the 'new' Sweden. This is the future of what this country must now be. We must therefore start in earnest a discussion about how we should today live our differences.

Swedish multicultural society

Alexandra Ålund

*Alexandra Ålund here analyses the complex
processes of transformation that have taken place
in Sweden in the 1990s, which have caused uproar
in a society once widely admired for its humane
policies towards its overseas-born citizens.*

The creolisation of world culture is reflected in its global cities, where variations are created which inspire visions of new possibilities. Thus, boundary-crossing and cultural fusion characterise Sweden, as they do other multicultural European societies. The relationship between social subordination, cultural resistance and the emergence of new cultural expressions and solidarities is a recurrent theme. And in Sweden's suburban communities, which are ethnically diverse as well as politically charged, you can expect to encounter a wide range of cultural developments with political undertones, expressed in text, tone and image. For instance, reggae and hip-hop exhort the listener to affirm solidarity, pride and self-respect; they also encourage demands for the realisation of equality, not surprisingly, since the development of youth culture in the multiethnic city is closely related to experiences of social exclusion.

Sweden is considered to be a multicultural society. However, today Swedish society is undergoing a division along ethnic lines. Social inequalities tend now to be understood in terms of cultural differences. Culture is then connected to ethnicity and race, and understood as something pure, an essence, related to some original and eternal ethnic core. This has meant that some important aspects of cultural dynamics in a multicultural society, such as cultural crossings and composite identities, are largely left unobserved. Within the framework of a multicultural society, new cultures, identities and ethnicities have been created. Departing from the problems of cultural essentialism which have been inherent in Swedish multiculturalism, we may draw the general features of the dominant discourse on ethnicity, its historical roots and relations to culture.

The concept of ethnicity, which has recently begun to loom large in the Swedish context, carries a lingering vagueness. It generally refers to group formation, and the drawing of both social and cultural boundaries between 'us' and 'them'. The old Greek word *etnikos* - which in ancient times meant heathen or savage, and denoted cultural outsiders - has, remarkably, retained much of its original meaning. References to the Others, the outsiders, those belonging to 'non-mainstream' cultures, or reckoned religiously as heathen, have been handed down over the ages, to the extent that the term includes the situation of the modern stranger in a multicultural society.

This static definition of ethnicity has - notwithstanding far-reaching criticisms of its limitations and consequences - become widespread in both everyday and institutional settings in Europe. This is no less true in multicultural Sweden, where public debate is marked - and hampered - by a static view of ethnicity. Reduced to something eternal, ethnicity is often associated, in particular in the Swedish mass media, with tradition-bound and foreign immigrant cultures.[1] Hence immigrants are considered deviant, and they are subjected to segregation and discrimination in almost every social sphere: including housing and work, child care and education, social services and health care. The focus on 'cultural' and 'ethnic' differences creates ethnically defined groups and distinct social positions. The collective appropriation builds on and promotes a hierarchical dichotomy between 'ethnic' and 'Swedish', traditional and modern. The concept of integration is associated with development, or modernisation. Cultural diversity is related in an ethnocentric manner to a superior 'Swedish culture', thus implying a 'natural order'.

The terms 'blackhead', 'foreigner' and 'immigrant' - with their attendant exclusion and cultural degradation - are related to the symbolic hierarchies retained in Swedish society. Discrimination in the labour market has made

---

1. For a discussion on the Swedish term *'invandare'* (translated as immigrant in this article), see note 1, p98.

Swedish people aware of the divisions within their society. There is no shared concept of what it is to be a 'citizen'; some are more equal than others. This represents the contemporary state and climate of multiculturalism in Sweden. Cultural encounters are stereotyped as conflicts between the civilised and the modern, and the primitive and traditional. The cultivation and polarisation of cultural differences adds fuel to the increasingly common political discussion about the levels of overall immigration into Sweden - both labour immigrants and refugees. Herein lies the basis for distinguishing between people, with selection based on purely cultural terms. In the long run this debate will be translated to the continental stage and serve to legitimise the idea of a 'Fortress Europe'.

The practice of multiculturalism in Sweden contains, and entails, a series of paradoxes that are associated with what has become known as 'structural pluralism'. This refers to a pattern of social inequality that tends to be explained in terms of culture and diversity, specifically where there is discrimination in the labour market that appears to provide evidence of an 'ethnic division of labour'. It is well known that immigrants with Swedish degrees have lower incomes than Swedes with similar qualifications. In the 1980s, qualified immigrants who had lived in Sweden since the 1960s often found themselves in jobs beneath their qualifications. Numerous studies have indicated that the children of labour immigrants are similarly disadvantaged in terms of their earning potential, and that this group suffers higher levels of unemployment than their Swedish counterparts. The 1990s have seen a drastic fall in the percentage of immigrants with jobs. Similar changes have occurred in relative income levels. Unemployment among immigrant youth is higher than among Swedish youth. Moreover it is substantially higher among children of refugee immigrants than among the children of labour immigrants. Hence, there is reason to view the trends of the Swedish labour market with alarm.

That a 'structural' rather than a 'cultural' pluralism has become popular in Sweden is indicative of the way in which migrants are viewed. While structural pluralism stands for the actual inequality of a vertically ordered 'ethnic mosaic', the latter term seems to have acquired a largely abstract meaning. Discrimination, in the labour market for instance, is made sense of through seeing ethnic groups as belonging to static and specifically ethnocultural categories, while cultural 'difference' accounts for the failure of minority groups to integrate.

The social dimension of ethnicity - its relation to class and status divisions, and to social segmentation and hierarchy - is obscured in talking of 'cultural difference'. In the multitude of cultural differences and clashes, culture is employed as a smokescreen to mask social divisions; inequality and segregation prevail. This cultural reductionism also helps to conceal underlying strains in the social construction of ethnicity and to reinforce a hierarchical status system. A complex and dynamic perspective on ethnicity, therefore, is necessary if the often-fundamental social conflicts associated with the cultural and the ethnic are to be rendered visible. All too often - in both social-scientific and popular discourse - the social dimension is overshadowed by culturalising stereotypes.

Culture is a result of human integration. It is rooted as much in social concordance as in material causes. The social and the cultural are variable and intertwined. Hence culture cannot be interpreted as a uniform and final product of settled symbols and meanings. Various experiences related to social positioning are mediated through cultural representations. These lie at the heart of the way an identity is formed among individual members of 'ethnic groups'. Ethnicity is thus a dynamic phenomenon, interwoven with ideas of class, gender and race. Neither culture nor ethnicity, then, can be defined as clearly delimited and internally uniform categories derived from an original source. The cultural constructions of reality spring rather from various sources and are spread through many streams.

The consequence of culture being considered as immutable obviously alters any discursive construction of 'immigrants'. The cultural boundaries formulated thereby are often based on an ethnocentric contrasting of traditional and modern, which then facilitates social stratification and the categorising and ordering of people along ethnic lines. It must be recognised that any notions of culture and cultural identity that are developed in multiethnic and multicultural contexts need to be reassessed in relation to migration. Cultural exchange is the manifestation of new identities, ethnicities and (political) solidarities. The anti-essentialist critique of research on culture and identity has led to a change of focus, from identity to identification, which in turn forms the basis of new solidarities and alliances.

In studies on youth culture during recent decades, the dynamic character of new cultural expressions has usually been related to class, generational conflicts, unemployment, social fragmentation, crisis of identity and to the global expansion of the market. Attention has been accorded to the development of composite social communities, which cut across ethnic boundaries and are articulated through new cross-border cultural systems of meaning. These function as collective self-confirmations on the basis of which alternative and authentic appearances on the public scene take form. Transcultural fusion into a form of syncretic culture acquires importance for both identity and community. In today's ethnically complex and politically charged environments, in the suburbs or inner cities of international metropolises, particularly those in Sweden, culture has acquired a new resonance and meaning. Expansive artistic developments among the young find avant-garde expression in text, tone and image, often with a political content, which initially mostly concerned anti-racism and the demand for equality and belonging.

Young Swedes with a non-Swedish background are still - even when they were born and raised in Sweden - referred to as 'immigrants'. In constructing an identification with Sweden, these young people challenge their current status as 'foreigners' or Others. It is for their cause that the constitutional recognition of a multicultural society is most important, since only a progressive process within such frames can realise a future democratic society.

The view from Sweden

Martin Peterson

Martin Peterson reflects on the prospects for the left in Sweden and in other West European countries.

The Swedish Model constituted for the best part of the postwar period a norm to which leftists in the rest of Europe used to refer, not least as an argument against shortcomings in their own nations. But the year of 1980 was in several ways a watershed even for this particular model. Its conception was in a basic respect dependent upon Keynesianism. However, the hallmark of the Swedish Model was that its ideological and technical architects had superseded Keynes in important respects. This had been possible because of the favoured position of the Swedish economy after the Second World War. Still, its whole approach, with a solidaristic wage policy as its main feature, was bold, and its explicit commitments to egalitarianism made it eventually highly vulnerable to pressure from global market forces.

In 1982 the last fundamental social reform of the Swedish Model came into being with the Social Service Act. In 1983 the first rift appeared in the previously solidaristic wage policy. The leaders in the wage-bargaining system, the high-earning metal workers, decided they were no longer willing to withhold their claims for the benefit of the lower-paid public sector municipal workers. That split became the signal for a general adjustment of the Swedish Model to globalising market forces. For a time, whilst the economy continued in good shape, no undue damage ensued. But as the signs of crisis accumulated, in the late 1980s, so the Swedish economy, and with it the Swedish Model, came crashing down. In the aftermath, during the 1990s, the Swedish left has swivelled between an adjustment to cosmopolitanism and to broad transnational solutions on one hand, and an extreme centripetal nationalism on the other.

The Swedish left is today groping with the same issues as the left in Germany, France and Italy. In fact, for some reason the left in the Latin nations have singled out the Scandinavian left as the new mainstream model. This is part of the ideological overhaul that the Latin left is in the process of carrying out in order to develop a more credible face. Delegations from both France and Italy attended with keen interest the recent congress of the Swedish Leftist Party which in recent years has shown much greater success at the polls, and indeed in actual policies, than its counterparts elsewhere in Europe. Among the new elements stressed were ecological issues and a new economic pluralism to counter unemployment. An openness to reorientations is evident everywhere, in spite of remaining rigidities such as the adamant commitment to nuclear energy on the part of the French Communist Party.

The Swedish Leftist Party has moved a long way away from its traditional Marxist positions. The previous leadership, which is still a presence in the debate, persists, however, in focusing on the concentration of ownership in narrow national oligopolies as the supreme social evil. On the other hand, the impact of the global intertwining of capital investments and ownership has shaped the outlook of the broad new generation of the left. This encompasses members of the Leftist party and the Green party, as well as the Social Democratic left, including new cadres of the trade union federation. This spectrum has the support of about a third of the population.

The ideological approach of the new leftist generation is concerned to find practical solutions which can make use of private capital and entrepreneurship to achieve social benefits and full employment. Obvious adjustments are being sought between leftist movements in Europe at the present time. The 35-hour week has now been launched as a realistic option in Sweden, for the same reasons as in Germany and France. In general there is a more acute awareness among Swedish leftist groups that supra-national harmonisation policies are necessary to achieve changed policies to enhance social justice and solidarity. Transnational flexibility in handling thorny elements of social policy could give the public sector greater support and authority. This is turn would make the role of governments easier, and strengthen the credibility of political solutions to social problems.

The representative organisations of the left have generally been more reactive than proactive during the past fifteen years. For example the European Trade Union Confederation (ETUC) was still putting forward 'offensive' programmes in the early 1980s. But since then its goals have been scaled down, confined to seeking marginal gains, for instance in the European Union's Social and Economic Committee, where it has promoted the idea of a Social Dimension. This programme came into being as a rescue measure on the part of Jacques Delors, when he realised that European labour had lost so much political ground since the late 1970s.

The passive and reactive qualities of the contemporary left reflect its recent spirit of resignation, and its settling for the view that it can at best act as a marginal protector of elementary values in a world ruled by brutal forces beyond moral control. It is necessary to make the implications and limitations of such a stance fully transparent, in order to challenge it. There are, however, certain specific areas in which the left has opportunity to develop offensive programmes again. These programmes need to reconnect with ideological discourses that assume an innate human desire to generate societal spaces in which creative human abilities can be fulfilled. Crucial is the development of the concept of solidarity beyond the level of basic needs to include higher levels of understanding and sensibility. During the last period of avant garde experiments - the latter half of the 1970s - when these familiar aspirations were still being articulated, the idea of providing space for creative capacities was slowly strangled by a neo-corporatist conformism, forcefully upheld by a still very Cold War.

In the remaining part of this article, I will identify some of the elements currently being debated in Sweden from which a positive left programme in Europe might be constructed.

The importance of human capital

The industrial policy of the Swedish Social Democrats was deeply influenced by, and gave some inspiration to, John Kenneth Galbraith's epochal work of the 1960s, *The New Industrial State*. Social Democratic governments have persisted in relying on Sweden's large flagship industries as if trying to fulfil Galbraith's prediction that economies of scale would not only make products more accessible but would also enhance the democratic element in industry, as technocrats took power from property-owners.

New conditions have made this perspective seem outdated. Regional networks, the 'new entrepreneurship', and the flexible economies of the 1980s diffused the openly adversarial relationship between capital and labour, and undermined the conflictual view of social groups in industrial society. Consensus policies and neo-corporate institutions had in the 1960s and early 1970s just contained vehement animosities in industrial relations. Conflict relations were built into industrial society at every level. Those arrangements were clearly felt by employers to be too costly to them, and they sought to escape their constraints by establishing more flexible relations to their consumer markets, geographically and in other ways. This enabled them to restore and indeed increase their powers to control their workforces. The outcome was the emergence of a new mode of co-operation - we might say enforced consensus - between capital and labour, focusing on the more efficient use of human capital. (The emphasis of the New Labour programme in Britain on skills and training is an example of this trend.)

The possibility of making something of this approach has now become a major point of departure for a new leftist strategy. This is now part of the political front line of the European left, which however now constitutes a much lesser threat to the established order than the disaffected grassroots of the impoverished unemployed and socially excluded, whom the organised left mostly fails to represent.

Among modern economists there is a conventional wisdom that the yield from human capital is much greater than the yield from machines and buildings in modern enterprises. If we make the rather unrealistic assumption that wages reflect labour productivity, the calculated sum total of human capital in Sweden was 10,000 billion Skr in the year 1990 if income after tax is used as the measure, and as much as 16,000 billion Skr if the measure is gross wages. This means that human capital has a value 7 to 10 times greater than the value of the physical capital stock in industry.

One of the major insurance companies in Sweden, Skandia, has during recent years tried to develop methods of valuing intellectual capital. In an international perspective, the USA is most advanced in this respect. According to one calculation intellectual assets (defined as the sum of individually-owned human capital, and other human capital owned by a company in the form of databases, etc) are on average worth three to four times more than the capital that is valued on the balance sheet (Thomas A. Stewart in an editorial in *Fortune* 3 October 1994). According to a further calculation, undertaken for the world's leading software company, Microsoft, these intangible assets have almost ten times the value of net tangible assets. This means that even in the most successful of knowledge-intensive firms there remain vast untapped human resources.

The most powerful administrators of human capital are obviously those who work in corporations. They in effect manage their own human capital, the content of their own brains. The yield from that capital is infinitely greater than the yield from machines and buildings. The fear of losing employees with special talents is today greater than that of losing any of the shareholders in a firm. The increasing role of knowledge is also weakening boundaries between firms. Firms cannot claim the right to own the thoughts of their employees. It is becoming more difficult to prevent employees from selling their knowledge to competitors. Hence the key to success for the modern firm is to transform individually-owned 'human capital' into the firm's collectively owned 'structural capital' - databases, networks, contacts with customers, etc. One key to success for a leftist strategy should then be to identify a way of deploying this accumulated human capital in a collective way.

Economic networks require administrators who select entrepreneurial individuals with whom they cultivate social relations such that they can judge what these 'entrepreneurs' are competent to achieve. Those who have the closest relations with these entrepreneurs are their colleagues in a firm. In the most modern forms of production, it is the knowledge-competence of the individual that plays the most crucial part. But it is also difficult to distinguish the individual contributions to collectively-owned structural capital. In modern firms within the fields of IT and biomedicine a major component is in fact team-work. In line with this thinking the left is arriving at a vision which is more-or-less that of the *Terza Italia* concept, which originated some decades ago.

Significantly, the Italian co-operative Basta, operated by former drug addicts, who become entitled to an element of capital ownership after specified years of strict toil, has been taken up as a positive example in Sweden. Similarly, regional networks set up on a voluntary basis in southern, western and central Sweden have been given much encouragement by the regional political authorities.

The use of pension funds

Another front-line strategy concerns the resources embedded in pension funds. This concept is far from new but some new ideas have unfolded during the course of the 1990s, coincident with a larger take-up of early retirement among employees, and the pressure to replace older employees with recruits from younger age groups. Pension funds are some of the biggest portfolio investors in market economies. At the same time that more people want to continue their professional work beyond the official retirement age, there is a growing interest in gaining access to a pension following early retirement. The development of varying attitudes to work in an age of unemployment indicates that flexible working-time systems, and more flexible approaches to retirement, need to be introduced.

The Canadian model of employee ownership and use of union-controlled pension funds for co-operative ventures is quickly gaining ground in the Swedish debate. The essence of the matter is to combine long-term investment by pension fund-holding owners, with short-term institutional programmes for employment creation. What is at stake here is the retention of employee belief in the value of the 'employee ownership' model, after five years in which there has been a sluicing away of trade union owned investment capital without any social purpose whatever.

The fact that major pension funds in European nations are by far the largest owners of capital, usually far superseding private monopolistic ownership, still appears to the grass roots as a rather abstract phenomenon. For instance, in the former socialist republic of Hungary, the first, second and fourth largest pension funds are at present controlled by Chilean companies, while the third largest is US owned. This type of selling-out to global capital, for want of experience and proper competence in eastern Europe, has demoralised the left in Scandinavia in regard to the possibility of making links with former Soviet bloc nations.

The fresh element in Sweden is a new use of pension funds by the regional trade unions for the setting up of regionally-based enterprises. In the Gothenburg area, the Social Democrat-controlled municipality has publicly encouraged the submission of proposals concerning the deployment of trade union pension funds. This goes against the stance of the national trade union confederation leadership, which remains highly hierarchical and centralised. The new idea of the political left, however, is to concentrate on the regional political framework. This implies that the new regional parliaments, in for instance the West of Sweden, should be given serious attention by union officials and radical parties alike.

Wage earner and local funds

The Swedish wage earners are already - directly or indirectly - owners of a very large part of the shares in industrial firms. Share funds and insurance companies are mainly built on savings put into them by wage earners. In 1997 two major pension funds owned together about 110 billion Skr. Among the unions the industrial white collar workers federation (SIF) owned almost 3 billion Skr in shares, and the metal workers federation almost 2 billion. The direct personal ownership of shares is however of little importance in Sweden, by international norms.

The core idea of the Swedish wage-earner fund proposal in 1975 was that employee co-ownership would lead to co-determination. This was intended to make it easier for wage earners to accept that a larger part of the accumulating value would go to investment and a lesser part to wages. The advisory council with more than 17,000 participants which took place within the Labour Confederation (LO) argued (unsuccessfully) that wage earner funds should be locally linked to individual firms, and not directed from above. The unfortunate development of the wage-earner funds is by now well known. Its major flaw was that the funds were not anchored among the grass roots of the labour movement. During the period in which they were active, the wage earner funds became mere common cruisers on the stock exchange. They did not contribute to any renewal of Swedish economic life.

Maybe the short and flawed existence of the wage-earner funds is one reason why the labour organisations are so sceptical about long term engagements of any similar sort. According to one newspaper report the white collar industrial union federation (SIF) is interested in profit-sharing. However SIF also prefers to invest in a multiplicity of companies and bonds, rather than seeking to invest in the shares of a single firm. Trade union spokespeople have said that they do not want to put all their eggs in one basket but rather to spread their risks. LO spokespeople have stated that they see their share ownership as in the first instance a capital investment, not as a means of exercising influence over the use of capital.

In other nations the question of a more active ownership role for wage-earner-owned pension funds has led to big discussions. In Sweden one of the leading architects of the Swedish model, Rudolf Meidner, has recently initiated a debate about the way that the Canadian trade union movement has actively used its pension funds in order to claim seats on company boards and to bring about an autonomous industrial policy. The issue of power over premium reserves in the new pension systems is about to emerge as a big bone of political contention.

In Sweden the left is trying to encourage as much local control over capital resources as possible. For instance, one of the most famous and starkly segregated suburbs of Stockholm, Rinkeby, which prides itself in having more than forty nationalities and as many languages resounding through its market places, is currently being encouraged to form a local capital fund, the 'Rinkeby Fund'.

New contexts, new approaches

A new dialogue has been established between the left and significant parts of the trade union movement, especially the local and regionally based ones. The central leadership in Stockholm still has too many vested interests in insisting upon a centralised line of policy and decision-making. There is more daring involved in a regional strategy, because of the unpredictability of its outcomes. The political left in Sweden is also making use of its improved contacts with continental leftist parties to develop its regionalist approach.

There are two other dimensions occupying the mind of the Swedish left. One concerns the public sector and its reconquest. Today the Swedish left encompasses a political spectrum consisting of innovative ideologues within the Leftist party, left-of-centre social democrats and regional trade unionists. It has observed how the public sector, the traditional domain of the political left, has slipped away from it. Other political forces are controlling it where it has any political life left in it at all. The two more conspicuous areas of the public sector that might be reconstituted are those of health care and education. The resources of both have been cut down severely. This means that client groups who ten years ago could be certain of having their problems or handicaps attended to are today left by the wayside.

Recently the European Commission asked economists in each member state to research what is the actual cost of unemployment. For Sweden the sum ran up to 153 billions Skr, which represented more than the cost of the entire health care system. The Social Democratic government has taken pride in its 'virtuous' slashing of the public sector. As a result of this, working environments in schools have become unbearable to the extent that teachers are quitting in droves; hospitals have slimmed down according to the ideals of 'lean production'. When figures giving the huge cost of unemployment were announced, the Government declared that as an initial response, an extra 16 billion Skr would be allocated to schools and hospitals. But on the very same day, a major hospital announced that it had to lay off a large part of its staff, in practice making it inoperable.

Faced with these contradictions of a public sector party in government, the left openly began to cultivate the idea that public policy in the interest of the people no longer could be confined within national boundaries. It would have now to be transnational in scope and content. This is a major concession on the part of a political movement that has hitherto been very sceptical towards European harmonisation, seeing a Eurocratic hoax behind every transnational policy approach.

The progressive left has now realised, in confronting the general psychological inertia in adjusting to the whole European system, that populist anti-European politics has been appealing to negative rather than positive inclinations. In March 1998 the OECD league table of national prosperity, measured in per capita GDP, once again revealed Sweden in eighteenth place. Finland, with virtually the same forest assets, and a similar telecommunication giant (Nokia) as Sweden (Ericsson), but which remains

'The wage earner funds did not contribute to any renewal of Swedish economic life'

vastly inferior to Sweden in its manufacturing industry, still remained ahead in the OECD list. Finland is a full member of the EMU and a very engaged member of the European Union compared with the half-hearted Sweden. The repeated explanation of the recent success of the other Scandinavian nations vis-à-vis Sweden has been that Sweden has acquired the 'British disease' in a new shape. Perhaps this resort to cultural explanation, previously unheard of in Sweden, was symptomatic of the rightward reorientation of the Social Democrats.

However, a progressive approach to politics remains high on the agenda in Sweden. This is despite the view held in other quarters that there can be no progressive politics without a successful economic policy that is fully accepted by the world market. A prominent member of the Social Democratic government put this view at a seminar in New York in April 1996. He might as well have said that he and his colleagues were content to sit on the laps of the big market players. But he was merely reflecting the mainstream stance of European social democracy, which nevertheless makes firm promises of a new dawn to come.

Multicultural society

Immigrant politics and the prospects for a Swedish multicultural society represent another dimension of Swedish politics.[1] It was the legacy of the Second World War from which Sweden had emerged with a doubtful reputation that made it important for an enlightened Social Democratic regime to develop a generous policy towards immigrants. This matched, as it were, Sweden's policy of solidarity with the Third World. In recent years, however, an obvious difficulty for liberals and for leftist political parties (which have the most genuine interest in the integration of the immigrant population), has become the volatility of the conditions in which immigrants live. The pace of industrial restructuring palpably accelerated during the 1990s. The high rate of immigrant unemployment has clearly added to the disarray and deterioration of relations between, in particular, the younger generation of immigrants and mainstream Swedish institutions.

The large networks of immigrant youth, that associate across ethnic boundaries because of their common experience of segregation and gradual ghettoisation, have now become a source of naked anxiety to politicians. These youth groups, as Ove Sernhede's article above describes, view Swedish society as another 'apartheid' entity. Their uncompromising attitude makes it hard to interest them in any party political work that implies subservience to established structures. A big issue is whether separate immigrant parties should be created, or if it still makes more sense for immigrants to work politically through existing political parties.

Recent incidents in the primaries to the Swedish General Elections have left a sour taste. The parties deselected some prominent immigrant politicians. In one case an immigrant Social Democrat, who for many years

---

1. For the term 'immigrant', see note 1, p98.

had publicly fought discrimination, was sacked by his own party. This was seen as ominous symbolic act. The fact that the politician himself may have been difficult to work with did not mitigate its significance. What is more, the politician concerned belongs to a powerful cultural group within the immigrant community, which could easily dominate immigrant politics if it chose to do so.

Many political refugee groups have reluctantly rooted themselves in Sweden. Of 60,000 Bosnian refugees given asylum only 1400 returned to Bosnia after the Dayton agreement. This is a new reality that has to be faced. A new state agency, the Integration Agency, was established during the early months of 1998 and its new head was appointed in mid-April.

Symptomatically, articulate immigrant opinion has raised two major objections to government policy. One concerns the failure of the Social Democratic government to appoint someone with an immigrant background as director-general of the Integration Agency. The other is a more general suspicion of its intentions, which are seen on the one hand as an enforcement of the idea that immigrants should become standardised Swedes and, on the other hand, as the institutionalisation of racial segregation.

In those suburbs of Stockholm and Gothenburg where immigrant density is high, more than forty different languages are spoken every day. According to one trade unionist and politician with a Chilean background, Nestor Vega, that is an argument against the formation of a separate immigrant political party. The risk would be too great, in this case, that representation would be monopolised by a single group whose political culture might provide it with an advantage, for example the Chileans in alliance with their fellow Latin Americans.

In the place of such a separatist strategy, the leftist political parties are making strenuous efforts to win the confidence of the young alienated groups. At political meetings in the suburbs recently, other socially excluded Swedish political groups have tried to use (some would say exploit) the immigrant issue for their own purposes, by making the entire affair into one of social exclusion rather than racial segregation. This is not to the liking of immigrant politicians, who prefer to portray themselves as political universalists, rather than as the advocates of separatist ethnic interests. Since the political left cannot afford to alienate any of these groups it is faced with a profound political dilemma.

Short-term action and long-term goals

The ideologically narrow and pragmatic games that most leftist movements in Europe are today playing lead them to adopt a tough-minded, realist approach to the constraints of the market economy. The idea is that political idealists must equip themselves with enough understanding of the business world (however little they may like its spiritual outlook) to prevent themselves being manipulated by it. There has been a related change in the attitude taken to small business. The vast mass of small defenceless entrepreneurs, who still in the middle of the 1980s were regarded as hopelessly backward by leading social democratic ideologues in Sweden, are now viewed as some of its chief potential supporters. The left is looking to this group to support its new pragmatism towards regional economic development according to the *Terza Italia* model.

The long-term policy of the left must clearly be to eradicate any trace of exclusion or segregation. In the short run, however, immigrant politics constitutes one of its greatest problems, since there is a growing awareness that this issue may not only decide the future of the welfare state, but also determine the credibility of leftist politics in general. It is becoming increasingly clear that, unless the foundation of the welfare state can be rewritten and designed with the multicultural society as its point of departure, the future of the left will put into serious question. This is not only true of Sweden, which stands out because of its history as an exemplary test case, but in most of Europe as well. The programme for such an adjustment to the multi-ethnic realities of the twenty-first century cannot now be written in one sweep, but must develop in stages as understanding grows. If it does not, the welfare state will be washed out, as will be the enlightened entity that we have come to know as the postwar nation state.